# THOSE TRACKS ON MY FACE

**Cliff Neville** began his career in journalism in the late 1960s, when he worked as a cadet with the *Sydney Daily Telegraph*. He then became a feature writer with the *Sunday Telegraph* before moving to the UK, where he was a London correspondent for the *Australian*. He returned to Sydney to become Chief of Staff of the *Australian*, and then went into television. Cliff is currently Supervising Producer of *Sixty Minutes* and it was during the filming of a segment with Barbara Holborow that he agreed to co-write her story.

**Janet Fife-Yeomans** is an award-winning journalist who has worked in newspapers and television in Australia and England. She has specialised in writing about crime and legal affairs for the past twelve years and is currently the legal writer for the *Australian* newspaper. This is her third book.

# THOSE TRACKS ON MY FACE

BARBARA HOLBOROW

WITH CLIFF NEVILLE
AND JANET FIFE-YEOMANS

William Heinemann Australia

Published 1997 by William Heinemann Australia
a part of Reed Books Australia
35 Cotham Road, Kew 3101
a division of Reed International Books Australia Pty Limited
Reprinted 1997 (twice)



Typeset in New Baskerville by J&M Typesetting
Printed and bound in Australia by Australian Print Group

National Library of Australia
cataloguing-in-publication data:

Holborow, Barbara.
Those tracks on my face.
ISBN 0 85561 738 1
1. Holborow, Barbara. 2. Judges—New South Wales—Biography.
I. Neville, Cliff. II. Fife-Yeomans, Janet. III. Title.

345.944081092

To all the children I have known and loved and all the people I have known and loved as we tried to get it right.

B.A.H.

# FOREWORD

Courts are fascinating places. They are a vitally important part of our judicial system, but they are also, in many ways, theatres where unscripted dramas are performed daily. The 'director' is the magistrate or judge, the players are real people, the plot often takes Shakespearian twists and turns. And it's all real.

Some of the most passionate and emotional dramas are played out in Australia's Children's Courts—the engine room of our juvenile justice system, where the pain and trauma of childhood and early adulthood are not confined just to those who are young. At some stage, just about every social issue and conflict will be addressed in a Children's Court. Up until now these courts have often been secretive places, forbidden to much of the public. But thanks to people like Barbara Holborow, this is now changing.

Barbara Holborow was a Children's Court magistrate in Sydney for twelve years. She was, before then, a solicitor specialising in young people's cases and in 1982 was appointed to the Bench. After four weeks' training, she was sent to one of Sydney's toughest Children's Courts—Minda—where she sat for three years.

Barbara was then transferred to Yasmar Children's Court for three years, before returning to the bearpit of Minda, where she served the bulk of her career. She then moved to Burwood and finally Campsie Children's Court. During that time, she saw from the magistrate's bench, life as few people have witnessed it. She saw the abused and the abusers, the pathetic, the humorous and the tragic. She had great moments and horrid moments, involving not only children, but also the adults who were their parents, their protectors, their friends and enemies. And she saw the system of justice, as it related to children. She despaired of its inadequacy, but was given heart by those she was able to help and is proud of having done her bit to help change some of the worst aspects of juvenile justice of that era.

At a time when the Children's Court was generally considered forbidden to public gaze, she opened up her court to the cameras of *60 Minutes* and mounted a public campaign to help open special gaols for young people who were too old to be locked up as children but too vulnerable to be incarcerated as adults. Partly as a result of her protest, Parklea Prison was rearranged in Sydney's outer west to cater for these types of prisoners. Her other dream came true in 1992 with the opening of Campsie Court—a court that deals exclusively with neglected children, rather than children accused of crime.

Barbara left the Bench in 1994 and is now an outspoken commentator on the rights of young people in particular, and victims of crime in general. In this, the first of what hopefully will be a series of books, she gives a personal account of what she experienced and felt while a magistrate. She also gives every parent the benefit of her experience of having held the lives of young people in her hands every day, in the hope that they may learn a little bit more about a world which, with any luck, they will never see first hand. Because of a complex set of laws about the publication of cases involving young people, this is what you might call a factionalised account. All of the people you meet appeared before Barbara in some way, but identities have been altered and, in some instances, cases have been condensed and combined to capture the drama of the court and minimise the tedium of which, she says, there was plenty.

Cliff Neville

# CONTENTS

CHAPTER 1

# A DAY IN COURT

GOD, I'VE had some good days and God I've had some bad days, but this day was very much one of the latter. I was sitting in my big tumbledown chair in what anachronistically was called 'my chambers' at Minda Children's Court and I really didn't want to be there. Outside my door was the Children's Court proper—a crowded and barnlike room more deserving of the appellation 'chamber'—and outside the court was a sad and stained corridor leading to what was known as the 'holding room'. Inside this 'holding room' was a selection of kids: white kids, black kids, nasty kids, nice kids, kids with baseball caps, kids with baggy jeans, those with crewcuts and those with long hair. A real menagerie whose only connection with one another was that they were kids. Kids bonded by trouble.

Mike was sitting on a wooden bench in one of two cells, down a passageway from the holding room. The shadow of the wire mesh windows played a noughts and crosses pattern on his white and green gaol-issue T-shirt, and he was staring at his toes. Dirty toes sticking out of a pair of green thongs. That morning Mike had been brought in a prison van from the remand section of Long Bay Gaol for his day in my court. He had a problem that most other kids would love to have: he had sensationally good looks, and in his gaol Stubbie shorts he could have been a southern hemisphere James Dean playing the role of an angry juvenile. I had been worried about Mike for the three days I had known he would be appearing before me, because what I thought I had to do with Mike gave me a power more awesome, more horrible even, than a judge who had to sentence an adult murderer to death.

'Ma'am, it's 10 o'clock. Are you ready?' Phil, the court officer, interrupted my thoughts about Mike with his usual, formal 'get on with it' reminder. He opened the door and I walked straight through to the chair behind a large cedar bench. While proceedings continued, the chair, the bench and I would be referred to as the Bench. The court was packed today; the usual mob of lawyers at the Bar Table, with a few I hadn't seen before sprinkled throughout the court. Good defence lawyers who hadn't seen me in action or weren't used to the peculiarities of the Children's Court would often sit unobtrusively at the back of the court like eagles in eyries, quietly observing the way things happened. After a few years as a Children's Court magistrate, you are able to observe pretty quickly what the day's going to be like and you can see all sorts of manoeuvring and goings-on in the court.

'All rise, please.' That was Phil's opening mantra and on cue all present did exactly that—about forty people rose to bow at me and I bowed back. Even though a children's court was supposedly less formal than an adult court, a lot of the formality stuck. And a lot of it stuck in my craw too, because it wasn't the ideal atmosphere to really communicate with kids, and I often enjoyed shocking those lawyers with a horsehair mentality by having kids up to the Bench for a chat. Anyway, on that day I have to admit I was preoccupied with the knowledge that young Mike was sitting in his cell waiting to see me, but there were other things to do first.

The police prosecutor that day was a constable called

Barry and there were two duty solicitors, Adriana and Peter, who shuffled their papers as they waited for me to start. Barry was dressed in his dark suit because, despite being a serving police officer, uniforms were discouraged in the Children's Court. Even policemen bringing kids straight from the scene of the crime were required to put on a civilian coat over their uniform—a rule which caused me to see a lot of scarecrows dragging screaming young criminals down the aisle.

'Okay, who's first?' This morning's list was a criminal list, which meant that the first kids to come before me were those recently arrested and in custody. We always dealt with them first because they had to be provided with transport and meals if they were going 'inside'—in other words, to a juvenile institution—and it wasn't a good idea to have them waiting around hungry.

'Ma'am, your first case is this young lady, Jocelyn,' said the prosecutor and through the door frumped Madam Jocelyn. Good looking in a mousy kind of way, this fifteen-year-old was trouble, perhaps not with a capital T for society generally, but with the T underlined and italicised for her poor, bewildered and desperate parents. She had been before me four weeks earlier on what was known as an 'irretrievable breakdown' under the *Children (Care and Protection) Act 1987*. This ground was introduced that year to be used by parents, or indeed children, when either party felt they'd lost control of the situation and needed something done urgently, and, boy did something need to be done with young Jocelyn.

It's never easy to sort out why things go wrong in a family. Kids who have a textbook upbringing screw up, and some of those who've been abused and led lives that one would think would wound them irretrievably, grow up as though there's nothing wrong. The Irretrievable Breakdown Order (IBO) at least gives the kids a chance to say what they perceive to be wrong and unfair and have their side heard by someone whose impartiality they should respect. I'm afraid, however, that kids quite often just see all adults as authority figures and view the courts and law as an extension of their parents' authority. It comes as a shock to them that sometimes their side is backed up.

But backing up Jocelyn unfortunately wasn't an option. She grew up on Sydney's upper crust north shore and went to a private school, but when she was thirteen her parents noticed that she would just disappear from home, first for a night, then for days.

She would wag school and a couple of times when her parents tracked her down she abused them in her best recently acquired and definitely un-north shore vocabulary. Then the police brought her home drunk. The parents arranged for counselling, which they all went to, but it did no good, and finally they decided that the only course was to apply for an IBO to see if a day in court would cause her to stop her heartbreaking conduct.

When Jocelyn originally came before me I had imposed strict conditions for her to agree to—no leaving home without permission, no drinking alcohol and an order that she attend school regularly. Of course she agreed; they all do. But it took her all of a week to break every one of those conditions and now she was back before me. This time her parents were not in court; the whole thing was just too distressing for them.

So here she was, draped over a seat behind the Bar Table, staring at the ceiling fan.

'I'm afraid,' said Adriana the duty solicitor, 'that she's back.'

I didn't take my eyes off the girl. 'So I see, and what have you got to say?'

A slight nervous tic and I could see that she was arrogant on the outside, but behind the arrogance there was still a fifteen-year-old.

'Will you answer me, please.'

'Yes.'

'Well, what happened?'

Now she was looking at me.

'I dunno,' and that was all she was going to say.

'Why did you get drunk again? Why did you take off again? Don't you just have one little bit of feeling for your parents?'

By now Jocelyn was looking down at the carpet and there wasn't a sign of a tear. I knew I could ask her questions all day and not get any further. She was working at being rude without the tantrums I knew she was capable of. This was her way to handle me, and she'd won because I was not prepared to use the weapons in my judicial armoury. There wasn't anything demonstrably wrong with the way her parents treated her, her behaviour was designed to get at them for a reason I would never know. There was no point in me seeking foster care in the short term because the carers probably could not do any more than the parents had done, and I wouldn't send her to a juvenile institution. She was the sort of person who would have her anti-social behaviour reinforced by the others in there, and there would be no doubt that she would emerge with a grab bag of new skills learnt from far more experienced practitioners of the art of juvenile bastardry. I was snookered and she knew it and I knew it.

I tried something. 'Joss,' I asked, and to this day I remember my words well, 'can you and I just talk directly to each other?

'Frankly, I don't know what's wrong … I don't even know if anything really is wrong. But on the basis that you're not mad or stupid, I'm saying to myself: "Why is Jocelyn running away?" You seem to go to a good school, have a good home, and as far as I know good parents.

'But Joss, only you can tell me what's wrong.

'And you're going to have to stay still long enough to be interviewed by a psychologist. If you feel the psychologist is not really listening to you, then tell your solicitor and other arrangements will be made. I know that there's really only one place where you'll be safe and well looked after and you know that's home.

'Will you promise me you'll think about what I've said and maybe we can get over this hiccup, because, Joss, that's all it is—a hiccup.

'Believe it or not as a teenager I had some hiccups in my life and some of those were doozies.'

She looked up at me as though I was from Mars and something to be pitied, shook her head slightly in wonderment and then curled her top lip into a sneer.

I thought, 'Barb, that little homily has fallen on deaf ears, but it was worth a try.' Only the next few weeks would tell how things would go. I had some confidence that there was light at the end of the tunnel because her solicitor was a mother and was wise in the ways of teenagers. She was sympathetic and understanding to her young clients, but she also rejected the nonsense they dealt out. She was always available to them, after hours included, and she would visit them in foster homes in Sydney's outskirts whenever they needed her, even though she lived in the inner city. She was on the duty roster for the kids who appeared at Minda Court, and she was one of the devoted ones. I'm happy to say that she wasn't unique, as you'll find out later.

There was nothing more to do, nothing more to be said.

'You can go now Jocelyn .... please try to remember your day here and what I said and what could happen to you—and think about your parents if you don't want to do something about yourself.'

And with that Madam frumped out of court the same way she had frumped in. I looked at Phil and he raised his eyes and I just shook my head and smiled. A smile, in this case, was a little bit of relief for the gut-wrenching frustration of having been able to do nothing. But I knew I would see her again.

'Number two, Your Worship, Ahmed.'

Ahmed again. He came into court smiling and with the kind of twinkle in his eye I had seen too much of recently. Ahmed was a chronic car thief. He just liked the things and he couldn't tell you why. He could break into and hot wire just about any brand of car and his count so far was over two dozen car theft charges. But Ahmed had another skill, or I should say two other skills. He was a chronic escaper, and as soon as he was locked up he'd be off again. His second other skill was that he could charm the uncharmable. He just had the type of boyish, sparkling face that made you like him. Ahmed played his three skills with considerable expertise. He once charmed five or so of his fellow inmates in Minda Detention Centre, where he was a semi-permanent resident, to escape with him. He arranged the escape time and route, and when they all turned up Ahmed wasn't there. He'd escaped though, but in a different direction, and he wasn't stopped because all the staff were busy stopping the other five who were trying desperately to escape using Ahmed's detailed directions. He once escaped from Minda by heading out the kitchen delivery door. He had charmed one of the hard-nosed kitchen cooks into allowing him to help her peel the vegetables, when normally Ahmed, with his record, wouldn't be allowed anywhere near an open door without an escort being present. When the inevitable had happened and Ahmed bolted to freedom, the Centre superintendent asked the cook why she had let Ahmed become her juvenile sous chef. 'I just couldn't believe that with a face like that he would do something so naughty,' she replied.

The police prosecutor read the charge and stated the obvious. 'The young person, Your Worship, escaped from custody while being taken from the Centre to the court. He is also charged with stealing two cars while he was out. He stole the first car because he wanted to visit his parents. He stole the second car because the first car had run out of petrol.'

Ahmed's Mediterranean blue eyes twinkled more brightly as these facts were read out, and I could feel, despite how much I tried to fight it, an embryonic smile in progress.

'I suppose,' I said, looking at Ahmed's smile now in full bloom, 'you're asking for bail.'

Ahmed thought the joke was hilarious, and pretty soon just about everyone in court except the police prosecutor had been caught up in it all.

'No,' said the young Houdini, 'not this time Mrs Holborow.'

'Okay, Ahmed, it's back inside for you. Bail refused. Set for mention on the 25th.'

As Ahmed was led away, I wondered if he would even make it back to detention today. His escort was the oldest and slowest juvenile escort we had and no-one was taking any special precautions. Normally, with a kid with his form, there would be police all around and the doors would be locked. But no-one, including me, had bothered because it just didn't seem possible. Ahmed had charmed us all again.

Ahmed had made a relatively bright inroad into a day that didn't have much levity about it. The next matter for mention wasn't going to help my mood at all.

Dimitri arrived with two policemen in tow, and his build, his swagger, his looks, his attitude, all spelled one thing—thug. He'd been charged with bashing a man in a local park the night before. He was being represented by Peter, the duty solicitor. There was a grey-haired, crying couple, sitting at the back of the court. Greek, I thought, and I had no doubt they were Dimitri's parents. These were anxious and confused people who were totally unable to help or comfort their child in an environment as foreign to them as Antarctica.

'You're charged with assault occasioning actual bodily harm,' said the police prosecutor.

I turned to Peter, 'Are you in a position to enter a plea today?'

Meanwhile, Dimitri looked so uninterested that his solicitor could have been answering a question about whether his client wanted mustard on his hot dog.

'No, Your Worship, I'm seeking an adjournment to obtain further instructions and I'd like to address you on the question of bail.'

'Your Worship,' Barry began, 'it is alleged that the young person and five of his friends set upon a man in his late forties in Lidcombe Park. They knocked him to the ground where they began to kick his head. While he was still on the ground and badly injured, they stole his wallet from his coat pocket and took off.

'A woman walking her dog heard the commotion and saw the defendant run past her. She found the man unconscious and called an ambulance. We still don't know whether this will be a murder charge because, in the doctor's description, the man's skull is like a broken eggshell. I ask that he be remanded in custody for fourteen days.'

I liked Barry's no-nonsense approach to delivering the facts. Some police prosecutors consider they're avoiding their duty if they perform with anything less than Rumpolesque flamboyance, but Barry was a straight shooter. The eggshell quote did the job. It even penetrated the boy's armoured steel body language, and he shook his head. It was the only emotion we saw.

These sort of kids often don't face the bloody consequences of their actions, and when they're confronted with it they are sometimes genuinely amazed at just how much damage they can do when they beat and kick and bash. The real world is not the world of the video store, which is where violence of this nature often starts, but the root cause of aggression is a complex business. My business, at this moment, was much more simple. Despite the protestations of Dimitri's solicitor, I refused bail, as I was about to remand Dimitri in custody for a couple of weeks for the police to prepare their brief. If it became a murder charge he would eventually be dealt with in a superior court by a judge.

I looked at this young man standing impassively. I looked closely to see whether there was a hint of guilt, a hint of emotion, but it was as though he were somewhere else. He had the eyes of a stale fish.

Dimitri looked down at the courtroom floor and then suddenly brought his head up defiantly as though he wanted his arrogance noted on the record.

'He was a bloody poof,' Dimitri hissed.

For a moment all you could hear was the sound of the boy's mother crying. I looked away from him.

'This matter is adjourned for fourteen days,' I said.

He'd be spending the time in Minda, but the prospect didn't seem to worry him. This boy who became a lion when kicking the life out of a man walking in a park was led lamb-like from the courtroom. His mother and father looked at him go and then looked at me, apologised and thanked me, but God knows what for.

I said to them, 'Have you understood what has happened here today and what I've done?'

The mother continued to sob, and as a mother myself I could have cried with her. The father said in very broken English, 'The detective told us that Dimitri has done something bad, but his mother and I can't believe he would do such a thing. He has three big brothers and none of them have ever been in trouble.

'He is not always a good boy but not this, not kick a man and rob him. I give him money when he asks for it. If he had needed money I would have given him money.'

Fortunately we had a Greek typist working at Minda and I asked Phil to take the papers and ask Julie to translate everything so that they knew what was happening.

The rest of the morning was taken up by routine. A parade of kids, some with their parents but most unaccompanied, plus their solicitors, passing in and out of the court like cars on a production line. And unfortunately, in many ways this court was a production line.

I went through the motions which had become second nature to me. A signature here, a stamp there, and an hour full of 'May I mention the matter of?' or 'I appear for'. Eleven-fifteen arrived before my mind had scheduled it.

'I'll take the adjournment now,' I said.

'All rise.'

I walked again through the door to my chambers, feeling dissatisfied and uneasy by Dimitri's case and thinking as well about the man who was in hospital because of him. I would know a lot more in fourteen days. How I hoped the victim would live. But who was really doing something about it? I can see why some people would be shocked by an attitude like Dimitri's, but the professionals who work with violent kids see it all too often and I couldn't let it upset me. I'd never spend another day in court if that sort of thing got me down every time it was raised, because the mindless aspect of juvenile violence was something that kept on cropping up over and over again in the years I spent on the Bench.

It wasn't Dimitri's case that was causing me to come to a personal decision which would eventually lead to my departure from the Bench. It was the certain knowledge that generally, our system of juvenile justice just about guaranteed that Dimitri, like so many others, would not really be helped. Now that he was on that conveyor belt the chances were he'd do it all again when he was freed.

My usual cup of tea arrived. Usually some of the Registry and court staff would come in for a chat. But not today. They all knew that Mike's case was on after the adjournment and that I was agonising about it.

Mike was one of those kids who the escorts called 'mate' because he was a likeable young man in his own way. He was still a boy, even though he was eighteen, and he had an innocent country charm about him. He also had a very bad record as a juvenile offender and had spent a lot of his childhood in detention centres, where he'd caused a lot of trouble. He was a kid who didn't seem able to help himself, who had a type of pride that caused him to react to situations with violence. He came from a small country town where his father owned a service station. I've seen a lot of bad kids where you could easily blame the sins of the children on their upbringing, but this was not one of them. The parents were confused and concerned. Mike's latest problem was that he'd tried to hold up a bank with a shotgun when he was seventeen. He had bungled the whole thing and panicked. The police found him and within a few hours he was back inside Minda. This time he was sentenced to more than five years.

In Minda he got into some minor problems, but it was clear that he was a disruptive force and the combination of this and his age caused me to defuse the volatile situation by having him transferred to the remand section of Long Bay Gaol and this whole situation filled me with horror. Without me making the appropriate order recommending he be sent back to Minda, it was likely he would be transferred to the main section of the adult jail.

Mike had a dedicated solicitor, Les, who with some sense of despair had followed his client's infamous career and faithfully defended him throughout it all. Juveniles in New South Wales are represented by solicitors paid for by the taxpayer through the Legal Aid Commission, a relatively recent development that has saved injustice to thousands of children of poor parents. But now that Mike was eighteen he was no longer entitled to juvenile legal aid. Les, on this occasion, was representing Mike largely at his own expense.

I finished my tea and looked at the clock and realised I could not put it off any longer. Back I went through that door, and once again there was the standing, the formality and the bowing and, even more than usual, I didn't want to know about it. The escorts brought young Mike in his gaol green shorts and thongs into the court and pointed to a chair behind his solicitor. Les, a kind, grey-haired man gave him a look which meant, 'Here we go.' I think I can truthfully say that Mike looked terrified.

'As Your Worship knows,' said Les, 'Your Worship has the power to allow this young man to return to the relative safety of the Minda Detention Centre from Long Bay Gaol, even though he is eighteen years old. There is provision for him to stay at Minda for at least the amount of time it could take for him to become somewhat more mature or, as I believe is the case under consideration, the authorities do something about separate gaol accommodation for people in Mike's predicament.'

This, then, was the crux of the matter. Mike looked very much like a young boy, and his behaviour was juvenile, although often violent. His problem was that the law made it very clear that he should go to gaol, not a children's detention centre, not for his crime, which was committed as a juvenile, but for the fact that he was born more than eighteen years beforehand.

The ideal solution was for there to be a gaol for eighteen- to twenty-one-year-olds, where kids of this age and adult first offenders could be kept away from the old lags who are nothing more than professors of crime with nothing better to do than to teach their art to their captive and often eager students. This was in 1989 and, despite much lobbying by lawyers and activists, the Government had not bothered to do anything about this problem. Things that often happen to good-looking boys in gaol defy description and their punishment can be worse than anything the law could do to them. Yet there we were, magistrates all but condoning it because of the system.

My mind drifted back to a case some months earlier involving Darren, a country boy who had been throwing his weight around in the detention centre and had been sent to

Long Bay Gaol for a few weeks. He appeared before me on the original charge that had sent him to Minda and I could feel nothing but pity for him. He was so close to eighteen and with his record there was no guarantee he would serve the rest of his sentence in a juvenile detention centre once he turned eighteen. His solicitor invited me to hear what had occurred and how Darren viewed his life. He had not actually been raped, but the constant taunts and threats of an impending rape had not only terrified him but appeared to have affected him mentally. Darren was not a sophisticated, articulate lad and I had no reason to doubt his story. He said that the other inmates called out things like, 'Don't go to sleep Darren, we're coming to get you,' over and over until he broke down.

As he was turning eighteen in ten weeks, I committed him for that period to an institution and the balance of his sentence was to be served on a strict bond for eighteen months. I had used the system as much as I could to stop the inevitability of rape. These young boys had to do time for their crime but not undergo this kind of intimidation. This was not, and still isn't how gaol should be for these young people. I was more determined than ever that someone should hear what was happening to these young men. I had cried in my chambers at the end of days when I had been forced, through lack of alternatives, to sentence a person to a period of detention which expired after their eighteenth birthday. I always added a recommendation that they be detained in a juvenile institution for the full period of detention. There was, of course, no guarantee that my recommendation would be accepted and I guess it generally wasn't.

But back to the present. Les went on, 'In the short time Mike has been in Long Bay Gaol, he has been threatened and propositioned so much that he has had to be put in the gaol's hospital section in isolation.

'Clearly, he can't remain there for much longer. Clearly, there will come a time when he will have to leave his hospital accommodation, which in itself is a punishment of solitary confinement, and be put in the main section of the gaol.

'And even if, in the main section, he is to be put into protection, his fellow prisoners in the protection wing have often been put there for committing the very offences they will no doubt wish to commit with young Mike.

'It is truly a very difficult situation that he finds himself in, and a terrible decision for you to make if you send him back there.'

As Les spoke, I was watching Mike's body language. I had carefully studied his record at Minda. I knew he was disruptive. I knew he was a bad influence on the younger inmates there. I knew that, even since going to Long Bay, he had been a problem. I knew that there was no real solution, no safe place for his body. Mike's parents had come down from the country for this very sad day. His father took his mother's hand as she dabbed and dabbed and dabbed at her eyes.

During all this, Mike was staring at his toes, and then occasionally he would look up at me, trying to establish eye contact. I tried to avoid him, but sometimes I would get a hint of a glint that I couldn't quite understand.

Les asked Mike to go to the stand and as he flip-flopped across the floor he looked so vulnerable, but when he got to the witness box he gave me a sort of smile—and I had a feeling that Mike was manipulating us all.

'What do you feel would happen to you if you were sent to an adult gaol?' Les asked.

Mike screwed up his face in disgust. Overacting? Sincerity? Who knows?

'There's homos in there. They'd rape you. There's other blokes in there that do other things to you. I've heard about them all.

'Miss, I'd prefer to be dead than to go in there with them blokes.'

'What would you do, how would you behave, if you got back to Minda?' I asked.

'I'd behave. I'd be good.'

As he trotted away from the witness box, I knew what I had to do but I didn't know how I'd get the words out.

I knew the situation inside Minda was like a powder keg. There were a number of boys bordering on eighteen and it would have only needed someone like Mike to light the fuse. Other kids, much younger and less experienced, would see him as a hero—having come from Long Bay back to Minda. There would be others who would want to challenge him. The problem I faced was weighing up the safety of a number of boys versus the welfare of one.

Maybe if I had been convinced that his behaviour had changed, that he had become less aggressive and violent, then I might have given him a chance. But I could see nothing of that. Everything in his records suggested he had a huge problem with violence and nothing indicated he had changed.

When Mike sat down on the seat behind Les I came straight to the point.

'I understand your problems at Long Bay, but unfortunately I can't be responsible for what is happening out there. But I do have a duty to the young people inside Minda and I believe you are still violent. I cannot let you go back, and for that reason the application fails.'

'Why?' Mike spat the word across the courtroom.

'Because,' I said, 'I don't think you've changed. I'm sorry.'

Mike just laughed. As he was led out of the courtroom he didn't bother to look back. I was left feeling a mixture of emotions, none of them good. Anger, mainly, at the system. Shame for what I had to do. A bit of doubt, but not much.

# CHAPTER 2

# ME

MAGISTRATES ARE appointed, not elected, and can reflect the good and bad of society. They're certainly not perfect. Some are atheists, some rampant Godfearers. There are bar crawlers, tearaways, leftists and rightists, good people, bad people and mediocre people. But I believe that the vast majority are professionals who want to do the right thing when you can't always define what the right thing is. When you're a magistrate, no matter what your lifestyle, when you arrive in the morning and sit on the Bench, you must throw your personal life into a psychological crematorium and behave as a dispassionate professional. Or so the theory goes.

My first day on the Children's Court Bench on 8 February 1982 was the culmination of a burning ambition to be a Children's Court magistrate. I didn't want to be any other sort of magistrate. It was the fulfilment of a less than finely honed dream to work with children. When I sat up there that first day I knew that I could contribute something, especially because of my career path, which was not in any way usual for such an appointment.

I wasn't one of those barristers who carried their books of learned wisdom and precedents to court in bags of red or blue slung over their shoulders. I came with a very different set of experiences and wisdom. My background thus far had been neither orthodox nor unorthodox, but my upbringing was not full of the sadness and lack of humanity which was often the burden of those who appeared before me.

There were some major events in my life that helped shape my attitude to those who were in trouble and, I hope, made me understand them more.

I was born in the area in Sydney in which I would later work—at Croydon Park on 29 June 1930 to Elsie and William Edmonds, and I was a baby they had never expected. They had lost two sons before I arrived and thought they'd never have another child. As their only and cherished one, my mum fussed and watched and I grew up feeling loved, but overprotected and stifled, especially in the difficult teenage years. My upbringing was generally cheerful and I spent quite a bit of time in the country. Most of my mother's relations in the city were musical, and they would come over to our brick bungalow with its huge suburban garden and sit around and sing to Auntie Vida playing the piano. Often Mum and I would visit my grandparents in Cobar, 800 kilometres out west. We'd leave Sydney's Central Station at 8.30 on Sunday night and get to Cobar at 5.30 the next afternoon. Grandad was a stock and station agent and we would go with him in a sulky when he did his rounds of the country properties, and through this I developed a deep affection for the country and its people.

Those were days I cherished, and days that I feel privileged to have experienced. I wish I could have passed on my own memories to some of those unfortunate kids who were to appear before me.

Mum and Dad would sit on the front veranda in the evenings in two cane chairs and have a few words for just about every passer-by. Every night the key was left in the door in case a relative or friend needed to come to our house. My father took me to the football every Saturday afternoon and we were passionate followers of Wests. As a young man my father had won medals for bicycle riding and he still loved the sport. We often went to the nearby velodrome at Camperdown and I would sit with him for hours on Liverpool Road when there were big, long-distance bike races, waiting for the riders to whirr past and then buzz into the distance.

I loved being with my father. I guess, in the way of those times, if he had had a son as well as me, then I would have been left at home while they did the manly, sporting things. I loved being treated as an equal in a time of extreme inequality between the sexes.

At thirteen, something ripped through my life like a hailstorm on a calm night.

I was enjoying life with two of the vital necessities of any newly teenaged girl—music and friends. Music was in the form of my piano, to which I was devoted to such an extent that I would practise without being told; and friendship came in many forms—the elderly people who lived in our street, the shop keepers I used to see regularly, my cousins who came to live next door, and, most unusually, in the guise of a doll called Elizabeth. I had acquired this special friend in the country many years beforehand and she filled in many hours for an only child. Every child should have an Elizabeth.

But then came the hailstorm—a burden which initially weakened me, but through my own pain, I became familiar with people who had the burden of pain, and in the way of these things, it gave me strength.

At first I had chicken pox, but then the little red lesions went on to become boils. Can you imagine being a young girl at a time in your life when you want your skin to be perfect, but finding it corrupted and awful to look at? In my case, in the days before proper diagnoses, the boils were considered to be a by-product of chicken pox, but they just didn't get better. At one count I had ninety-nine of what they called blind boils and was in bed for months. Each boil had to be lanced with surgical skill, and at the one time I was both a sick girl and a lump of medical lard which was nicked and nicked and drained and mopped and wiped. I was so weak that I couldn't walk across a room without resting. But the strange thing was that my appetite was ravenous. I ate like a famine victim and drank water like an alcoholic with a constant hangover.

The doctor couldn't figure out what was wrong and my parents were despairing. In desperation they sent me to Bowral, with my nana, to see if the country air would help. My nana was anxious to help me, but I just moped and cried and I was desperately ill and confused. I would eat and drink and still nothing would get better. There was no real time for school and there was no real time for living. It was an unholy netherworld that, as a teenager, I felt angry and bewildered about. But there was nothing Nana or I could do about it.

On a sultry Sydney day in April 1943 the steam train pulled in to Strathfield station with my country get-well holiday delivering me back to Sydney in a far worse state than I had started. My mother met Nana and me at the station. She took one look at the pale and skeletal creature who was dragging the big blue suitcase down the platform and burst into tears. It's funny how you remember things, but I remember my biggest and most heartbreaking agony at the time was that I wanted my mother to be aware that I wasn't looking like this on purpose; that I would do anything to change the situation but I didn't know how. I wanted her to know that I hadn't done anything wrong, that I desperately wanted this cloak of sickness lifted so that we could relive the old times again, with her and Dad on the porch and the music and the nights of happiness.

Mum took me straight from the train to a doctor she had heard about, a man who had some expertise in diagnoses, as distinct from just being able to patch up and prescribe. This doctor had his surgery opposite the Western Suburbs Hospital, and he took one look at me and then asked Mum a lot of questions.

'I think,' he said 'that she might have diabetes. She's in a very bad way and we've got to get her across the road into hospital. Take her home, pack her pyjamas, and get her to Western Suburbs. Quickly.'

At the hospital they confirmed the diagnosis.

Diabetes.

It was a word I hadn't heard before. In those days, it wasn't quite a death sentence, but it was close to it and it was something that no-one wanted to know about. I had never seen my father cry before, but when my mother told him, he lay his head on his strong brown arms and wept. His younger brother had died from the disease before insulin had been discovered, and the word brought back all those memories. He was certain he was going to lose his daughter, his 'chick'.

Three weeks after going in to Western Suburbs hospital I walked out as a relatively well young girl, but my medical passport was a syringe and needle and my visa for life was a constant series of injections and monitoring of blood sugar levels. One afternoon, I was feeling very sorry for myself and sat crying in my bedroom when my nana came in and asked what the problem was.

'I don't want to be a diabetic,' I got out between the sobs.

'Well you are, and you can just sit there and cry for the rest of your life or get up and live,' and with that, she turned and walked out of the room.

From that day, I never let my diabetes come between me and what I wanted to do. Those few words of hers had a profound effect on my life.

When it came to the injections, my mother wasn't capable of sticking needles into me and, for that matter, nor was I. There was a radiographer up the road, and he agreed to inject me every day. Each morning I would trot up to him for my needle, and after a while all the subcutaneous fat disappeared from my thighs from the constant injections into them.

I loved swimming, but I was too self-conscious to allow anyone to see my 'deformed' legs. If I had told Mum what was wrong, she would have suffered my humiliation for me and I guess this is where my independence came from. One Sunday afternoon, I walked to the casualty department of the Western Suburbs Hospital, just two streets away. I explained my problem to a young registrar and his advice was straightforward, 'Well, stick it in your stomach ... and if you are too afraid to do that, then stick it in your bottom.' That was it for me. If I was going to have a needle stuck in my bottom it was going to be me who did it and not the radiographer up the road. It was then I started to feel like a teenager again.

Diet is a major part of managing diabetes, and I was considered a curiosity among my friends. When they ate sweets I'd have Sao biscuits as I couldn't drink or eat or do many of the things that kids wanted to do.

But I survived all these things and my parents were, in fact, more drained by my diabetes than I was. Emotionally, I felt I had conquered it, but not so my parents. I often remember hearing, 'She's got diabetes you know' whispered as an excuse when an excuse wasn't necessary.

School was a turmoil, and while I was good at some parts of schoolwork I just didn't feel as though I wanted to be there. I did, however, have some great friends, and one special friend, Moo, is still my buddy. I had lost a lot of days from school, my schoolwork was beyond my parents and they couldn't help me, and it all became too hard. In fact, the most memorable day of my school life was when a plane carrying two very young English pilots clipped the bell tower and crashed across the road with a huge bang. I remember thinking that this was how it must have been in England every day during the War.

I left school at fifteen. I felt that I could have gone on quite easily, but Mum really thought I was too weak to do it, and she thought I should try to get away and do something else. I had a great number of friends who attended the same church, most of us were in the choir, and I taught Sunday School. I would take my class of young kids to the zoo, or to Manly, and Sunday became my favourite day. This is when I became particularly interested in kids who were deprived of an upbringing that most of us took for granted. Some of the kids who went to our church were from a boys' home called Milleewa, then in Ashfield, and they were from so-called broken homes. Even though I wasn't much older than most of them, I went to dinner at Milleewa once a week. I also taught them music, and we formed a little choir. At Christmas we always had one or two of the boys stay with us for what my mother called a 'proper Christmas day'. I used to visit another children's home, Weldon Street, with a bag of lollies each Saturday, for those who didn't have a parent visiting. Although I couldn't articulate it in those days, I became interested in their welfare, an interest that was to possess me for the rest of my life. It is paradoxical that a good part of my life would be spent dealing with kids who are dishonest, because I think the thing that I love most about children is that they are all basically honest. They laugh spontaneously, they cry when they are hurt, they have secrets which they love sharing. Until, inevitably, they start becoming adults.

I met John Holborow at Sunday School at the age of nine. Ten years later he invited me to the Fort Street ball because his date was away. After that ball, neither of us dated anyone else, and John and I were inseparable. John had been raised by two elderly bachelor uncles and a spinster aunt and a wonderful cousin whose husband had been killed at the fall of Singapore.

I played basketball, John played cricket, we played tennis each Saturday morning. We went to a lot of first nights and many balls and did all those wonderful, innocent and, compared with these days, conservative things that teenagers did in the forties. We weren't quite Fred Astaire and Ginger Rogers, but you get the picture. We had a wedding that most young people would envy, with no expense spared, and we took the Sunderland flying boat from Rose Bay to Hayman Island for our honeymoon.

We didn't think anything could ever go astray with our relationship. But pretty soon *Mills and Boon* would turn sour. Relationships tarnish for a lot of reasons. We lived on the top floor of a terrace in Croydon owned by John's mother and my life became a constant parade of relatives. John's uncles, his mother and my parents were always wanting to come around or for us to go to dinner. John and I seemed to be trying to please everyone and we had no life alone. One of the lessons I learned painfully is that most young people need freedom. They need to be away from people who, for whatever reason, need to possess them. People are not possessions, they need to live, breathe and exist as individuals, and most people hate being stifled. By the time I was six months pregnant, I was very unhappy. I 'knew' my baby was a boy and I spent a lot of time speaking to him and would go on long walks chatting to my unborn son. My health was once again a concern. Pregnancy in severe diabetics is a tricky business, and in those days in Sydney, there weren't many doctors competent to manage it. No-one had told me to be concerned for the health of our baby (whom we had decided would be called Kim) and when I went into hospital I fully expected to be walking out with our little Kim. I was, of course, also hoping that Kim's birth would bring me, and our marriage, back to the days when happiness was the norm and not the exception.

Kim was born on 11 May 1954 to silence in the delivery room. Then after a while a nurse said, 'What a pity.' Those words ripped into my heart.

'What is it, what's wrong?' I remember myself asking, in a voice that wasn't really my own. They told me, simply, that he hadn't survived.

They wrapped Kim up in newspaper and took him away. I saw the nurse doing it and I screamed, 'Don't do that to my son!' My son was removed from my sight and my life but not from my mind. And that's one of the reasons why I can empathise with women when I remove their children and, in my view, when a child is removed from its mother and made a state ward, she should receive grief counselling, because the loss can be worse than a death.

In those days there was no grief counselling. I was unceremoniously wheeled into a ward with unmarried mothers whose babies had been removed, 'so I wouldn't fret', and I cried every night. One thing, however, did help. A sister saw me crying and came in with a baby and said, 'Here, hold him.' I took the baby in my arms. It wasn't Kim, but somehow this little, anonymous boy, who would be in his forties now, passed something on to me and I felt I could cope. The mothering instinct is so complex in humans, and indeed in animals generally, that we really can't explain why things happen. But holding this baby stopped me crying and the message this little guy was sending me was, 'Get on with it, Barbara. Get on with life.'

John and I continued our uneasy marriage and the following year I was pregnant again. This time I sought out a specialist who knew about managing diabetes in pregnancy and I spent the major part of my pregnancy in St Luke's Hospital. Despite all this care, I suffered haemorrhages and lost the sight in my left eye, but on 18 November 1955 life worked its magic and Louise Elizabeth Holborow was born.

Louise spent the first few days in a humidicrib and I was so weak I couldn't pick her up, so someone had to place her in my arms. When I was allowed to hold her for the first time I don't think I have ever felt such love. I could physically feel it running through my body like hot blood. I was immortal. I lived in her and would go on living through her and her children.

Our marriage continued to deteriorate and after two years I had to get out. I was in a horrible emotional mess and I hurt John terribly. We separated in January 1958 and I knew that my life had to make a dramatic turn if I was to be faithful to my own abilities and take care of Louise properly. We went home to my parents, and I got a job in a local law firm, C. A. Mitchelmore and Co., in Burwood. I worked as a legal stenographer, which I had been trained in before I was married. Mr Mitchelmore had just branched out on his own, and we worked hard and expanded. The firm grew and grew and before I knew it we had nine people busily typing away, more cases than we could handle, and I was known as Managing Law Clerk. I loved it so much I decided to study law, but first I needed my Leaving Certificate. So off I went five nights a week with other mature-age students to Burwood Public School to study. I got my Certificate in a year, then the following year I enrolled at university.

Two nights a week I went to Sydney University and studied for the Solicitors' Admission Board. I took all the notes in shorthand, came home, had dinner, typed up the notes and went to work the next morning. I studied from my notes at work, in between what I was doing for the company, and I had the wonderful advantage of having a very understanding boss who wanted to see me succeed. In what seemed to be an instant, Louise had turned ten and I was well on my way to becoming a solicitor, and working very hard.

At weekends I would study with two 'soul brothers' and every six months we would sit an exam. It seemed that no sooner was one exam over than another had begun, but I was working furiously and enjoying it. I used to go to bed at 8.30 at night and then get up at 1.30 a.m., study until 6 a.m. and then go to work. At weekends, to make a little extra money I would sometimes 'run' for the bookies at greyhound race meetings. I don't know how I came by the job, but I found myself scurrying around race tracks offloading extra money between bookmakers, and soon I knew just about every bookie and every dog and got to know a lot of wonderful characters. It was a new and earthy world which I can still smell and feel and which introduced me to a wonderful side of life.

I graduated with a law degree in 1969 and was admitted as a solicitor, and Dad and Louise came to the Supreme Court for the ceremony. They were in a hire car and bursting with pride, and, I've got to tell you, so was I. I was a battler, and emotionally and medically, I'd had a hard time. But here I was reflected in the gloss of the Banco Court's handsomely polished mahogany, surrounded by Their Honours. It was not an easy time to be a lawyer and a female as well, but I was determined to give it a go.

I branched out on my own and set up a practice in Glebe, a bustling, working-class, inner-Sydney suburb buzzing with university life, Glebites, pensioners and a fair share of criminals. I found a small shopfront at 4 Glebe Point Road that I rented for $10 a week, and I discovered that I was Glebe's only practising solicitor. When my $1000 savings ran out, so, I thought, would I. The Glebites seemed to take to me, however, and I got a lot of varying work, but I couldn't bring myself to charge pensioners.

I also got some very lucrative jobs. The people of Glebe used me instead of a Department of Main Roads solicitor when their properties were being purchased by the department for a freeway through the area, but most of my work was with people who could barely afford to support themselves, let alone pay hefty legal fees. My payments were sometimes in peas or a cake or scones, and sometimes I suggested a 55c lottery ticket would suffice.

I encountered lots of characters and laughs in Glebe. One of my first meetings was with the Delaneys, a family of minor criminals who were almost always in trouble. Car stealing was pretty rife in their family, but after I had represented the two youngest boys on minor theft charges, the word went out that no-one was to lay a hand on Mrs Holborow's old Cortina. I could leave my car unlocked in Glebe or Newtown or Annandale and while securely locked cars parked in the same street would be deftly stolen, mine stayed intact. There was always conflict between the Delaneys and the local police. One of the problems was that the boys, like their father, could not say it was a good day without saying it was a good fucking day. It was a convenient charge for the police to lay against the family. The Delaneys were always up for offensive language, and with the offensive word, according to the police, always being said in the presence of women and children. Men were, of course, strong and would not be offended, but the mere mention of such a word near women would make the fairer sex swoon. Until I came along, the Delaneys had always had a male solicitor, and my first appearance in Glebe Court on an offensive language case caused much wriggling embarrassment for the prosecuting sergeant. How could he say the word in front of a woman if our gender had this frightful reaction which would bring down the full force of the law on those unfortunate enough to be caught saying it? The sergeant tried to say the word several times, but years of conditioning had prevented him.

'Come on, sergeant, say it,' I said. 'If fuck doesn't cause me any consternation, then I believe that my friends at the Bar Table will be equally unconcerned.'

I called young Wally Delaney to the witness box, and questioned him minutely about how, when, where and why he had used the word, using it myself as often as I could. Wally got into the spirit of things and, after a quick and nervous glance at the sympathetic magistrate who was also sick of the police using this charge to get the Delaneys into court, he was away, and the courtroom was positively purple with unseemly prose. That colour is also appropriate to describe the hue on the face of the beleaguered prosecuting sergeant. I am glad to say that the Delaneys were never charged with offensive language again, although their use of it as a universal adjective did not diminish.

At that time I became very involved with children's court work. In May 1974, the Law Society introduced free legal aid for children, which meant having duty solicitors at each Children's Court to represent those who could not afford legal representation. Before then, kids whose parents were able to get a lawyer to represent them were the lucky ones, as many of the most deserving and often inarticulate kids were left to their own wits. If they had a caring and sympathetic magistrate, fine; but the problem was that those qualities were not always to be found in some of those who were to become my judicial brethren. I joined an informal group of like-minded solicitors and was appointed a duty solicitor for the Children's Court. All of us worked tirelessly to keep kids out of institutions in all but the most obvious cases. At this time, kids could be institutionalised for truanting and it went against my grain. My constant work with kids meant that I had to expand my practice and employ another solicitor, because I was never in the office. The Law Society was sending me to country towns and the expense to the practice wasn't recouped with the fees paid to me. My parents were elderly, and I, as an only child, was their sole support. I was paying for them in a nursing home. Additionally, while I was a solicitor, there were seven children whom I took in as 'foster' children, but more about them later. Looking after growing kids, however, costs money. Quite frankly, I was slowly going broke. I got back to the office one day and Glenda, the other solicitor, and the staff confronted me, in the nicest possible way.

'We need to talk,' Glenda said. I knew it was serious.

'Okay,' I said, 'Let's shut up shop and go to lunch.'

Armed with a credit card, we headed off to the Italian restaurant down the road and over a bottle of Frascati they came clean.

'We've worked out we can't afford you,' said Glenda, 'Do you know you've only brought in $8000 with all the kids' work in the last year. You're never charging enough and we'll just go out backwards if you continue running the office.'

From that day Glenda started running the office, and it suited me down to the ground. When it came to kids, as much as I knew it was not good business, my soft heart overruled my financial head.

Shortly afterwards in 1981, I was able to combine both head and heart when I received a telephone call from a friend telling me there was an ad in the *Sydney Morning Herald* for the appointment of a Children's Court magistrate. They were taking people from outside the public service, and would I be interested? Would I! It was a new trend to appoint from outside the public service. The position had been advertised within the bureaucracy, but no-one had sufficient experience in Children's Court matters. This did not, however, stem the feeling of disquiet that private solicitors were about to infiltrate the hitherto sacred Petty Sessions domain. I was interviewed by a committee of men in the city. A bride could not have taken as much trouble or gone to more expense than I did for my 'interview outfit'. I remember that Clarrie Briese (known, of course, as 'Seabreeze'), then the Chief Magistrate, was one of the interviewing committee. He was such a gentle man and soon put me at ease with his great smile. Once I was asked questions about the Children's Court I felt very relaxed and at home, because I knew I was really in control. None of the interviewers had spent as much time in that court as I had, nor were they as up to date with the cases.

Then came the waiting. I was hoping that I would know before Christmas, but November went and so did December and still no word. Rumours were flying. One I found very worrying was that a woman had been chosen and when considered by some senior executive he had been heard to say 'no way'. Finally I was advised 'that with great pleasure etc etc. …' It was me! One of my staff, Maria, who had been with me at Mitchelmore's since she was fourteen, gave me a silver gavel to hang on grandfather's watch chain. That gavel has never been off my neck since 14 January 1982.

A couple of weeks later, before I had taken up my duty officially, I was invited to attend a dinner for a retiring magistrate, a function which just about every other magistrate in Sydney attended. Some made me welcome, others didn't. The judiciary always referred to each other as 'brothers'. So I went up to one magistrate, before whom I had appeared for years and said, 'I haven't said hello since I became your sister.'

'I'm an only child,' he said, 'I haven't got any sisters.'

The retiring magistrate made a speech, in which he said, 'I do not believe that positions should be available to any person, qualified as a solicitor or not, who has not come through the Public Service.' Too bad, buddy. Even those old fogies failed to dent my delight in the appointment. My staff were wonderful and so happy for me. We called ourselves the Stars of Broadway, because Broadway was the name of the main road near our practice in Glebe, and all the Broadway Stars, and the real stars, were shining for me.

My first day on the Bench at Albion Street—a rambling, Dickensian children's court in inner Sydney—was a treat. I walked through the door and looked down for the first time from the seat I had looked up to so often and saw my chance to make things different, to actually change some of the things I knew were wrong with the system. I knew I came to the Bench shaped and styled by human experiences, not by academia or the Public Service, but by life itself. As I sat down to my first day on the Bench I looked at the big mound of papers waiting for my attention. I laughed. I didn't have a clue how to fill them out. Maybe the fogies had been right. Maybe you had to go through the Public Service just to learn how to fill out the forms.

CHAPTER 3

# 'WHO'S GOING TO CLEAN THE SWIMMING POOL?'

IN MANY ways domestic violence is a disease, with much of the characteristic pathology of a disease. It traumatises and disfigures and is sometimes fatal. It is often hereditary and, tragically, it can be highly contagious. When an adult bashes their partner, they probably have no idea that they are at the same time bashing hell, psychologically, out of their children. And it's a sad fact of life that many children who are products of domestic violence go on to become wife- or child-bashers. I was pretty much insulated from many of life's horrors when I was a girl but, boy, did I make up for it in my years on the Bench! The variety of those who practised domestic violence never ceased to amaze me. They crossed every cultural and professional border, and it's true to say that a man in a blue pinstriped suit can batter just as hard as a man in blue overalls. Let's talk about a case in point—Ismelda Young.

'Ismelda,' said Steve. 'Not her again.' Steve and I were going through my precourt lists, which were piles of white, green or yellow papers all in cardboard folders stacked on my desk. Steve was a nice bloke, he was my sound monitor and we often went through the list together so we'd get an idea of what was in store. On this particular day Steve was giving me two rundowns—one for the court and the other of his winnings on the race track. Steve never had much money to spare, but if there was anything he loved it was a flutter on the horses, even though his girlfriend didn't quite share his enthusiasm for the sport. Magistrates' courts had finally given up on the laborious job of using clerks to thump away at ancient typewriters in an attempt to faithfully record the day's proceedings. In Minda, Steve sat behind a table groaning with sophisticated recording gear. There were microphones for the witness box, the Bar Table and me, and by wearing headphones, Steve could electronically make audio indices that separated the various cases. The tapes would then be sent away for transcription if necessary. How quaint are the ways of paradox, as while many of the institutions for kids in trouble were overcrowded and Dickensian, the means of getting them there was very much state-of-the-art indeed.

You could tell by the state and weight of the cardboard folders just how much each child had had to do previously with the court, and Ismelda's was pretty heavy and dog-eared. I thumbed through it yet again. She had come before me three times previously after running away from home. But each time, when I had asked her what was wrong at home, she would just shake her head and mumble. I had adjourned the case until today and I was determined to get to the bottom of it all. She was before me as a 'care case'. At Minda, we had special days set aside for care cases, where generally there were no criminal charges involved, but there was concern for the welfare of a child. In some ways these were more difficult than criminal cases where at least you had the black and white of the word of the law to guide you. With care cases you had to identify the problem, judge the extent of the threat to the child and then decide what to do about it. You could decide to leave the child at home with special conditions, send them to foster care or, in the worst cases, make them wards of the state. It was a big responsibility which often caused me sleepless nights.

I walked into the court and my clerk declared it open for business. Issie was there with her mother, younger brother and sister, and the four of them sat behind a barrister, hired by the father, which put me on notice. It costs quite a lot of money to brief a barrister. You don't see many of them in care cases, and I felt he was hired not so much for Issie's benefit, but for her father's protection. Dad was, in fact, conspicuous by his absence. So conspicuous in fact, that I repeated this old cliché to myself.

Issie was fourteen and had every reason to be happy. She lived in a big house in Sydney's eastern suburbs, her father was a leading businessman who had been in court for Issie's previous appearances.

'Where's the father?' I asked the barrister.

'Unfortunately, Ma'am, the pressure of business. He just couldn't get here,' he said.

'Uh huh, I see.'

The barrister started to outline the basics of the case and was a bit startled when I interrupted.

'I know all this,' I said, 'Issie has been here quite a few times before. I want to address a question to Mrs Young.'

The barrister turned and motioned for Mrs Young to stand. She was a perfect example of a groomed and rich lifestyle. Hardly a hair where her hairdresser didn't want it; her lime green dress and matching scarf no doubt coordinated in some Double Bay boutique. She looked both sad and nervous at having to talk to me. Perhaps she had hoped the barrister would do all the talking, and in some courts he might have. But not in mine.

'Mrs Young,' I asked, 'What would you like to happen today? What can we do to stop this heartbreak for you and Issie? Please just tell me what you see as a solution.'

'I just don't know what to do,' and the tears shone in her pale blue eyes, 'she is never home. I just want her to come back. There are house rules, but I don't think they're too bad. We've got a lovely house and a lovely pool and she could have anyone over that she wants to. But she just stays away. I don't know …'

Suddenly Issie was on her feet. The barrister half rose to try to stop her, but it was too late. Issie's face was now only centimetres from her mother's and she began to shout.

'Mum, bloody stop it,' she was crying, 'tell Mrs Holborow the truth. Tell her how he drinks and drinks and how he hits you and shouts. Tell her how we can't stand it. Tell her how he told you to shut up about it all. Go on, tell her.'

So this was the truth behind Issie's behaviour. This was why she had run away all those times. Finally we had got to the heart of her problems.

Issie slumped back into her seat. Her younger sister was also crying, but the brother was glaring at me, wishing this whole thing would just go away. Mrs Young was now sobbing and the barrister was looking a little breathless. I decided to send them outside to compose themselves and so the barrister could receive fresh instructions.

As they were getting ready to leave I addressed them. 'I think,' I said, 'that it would be a very good idea if the father gets here.' I said it in such a way that everyone realised that I meant it.

I dealt with a series of minor matters while I waited to see what would happen. After an hour or so they filed back into court, minus the barrister but with the father in tow.

The barrister's place at the Bar Table was taken by his instructing solicitor who, upon my inquiry, advised that the father had fired the barrister. A tough businessman indeed.

'Okay, let's get on to resolving this,' I said. 'Mr Young, would you stand.'

The father stood up revealing a dark and expensive suit, blue shirt, red silk tie, matching silk handkerchief and a floridly handsome face.

'Sir,' I said, 'It would seem to me that from evidence given this morning, admittedly unsworn evidence, that if I am to heed that evidence Ismelda may have had a very good reason for running away from home. Do you want to comment?'

The father cleared his throat. He was calm and sure of himself.

'My wife and I have our differences. Every couple does. But their children don't keep running away. I refuse to go looking for her one more time.'

I could have got very heavy indeed, but I thought I might try a softer approach.

'Yes I understand that,' I said, 'but let's get to the cause of the problem. The important question you should be asking yourself and talking to your wife about is: what is going to be done about the home situation while the children are there?

'This is really getting quite bad. You can see what effect it is having on Ismelda. Heaven knows what it is doing to your other children.

'This is what I think. I think you and your wife need counselling and probably time out from the current domestic scene. I ask you this: would you be prepared to move out for a time until some of your differences are resolved and the tension is reduced with professional help?'

He thought for only a minute. He knew that if he was going to be difficult, I could be too, and the whole question of his violence would be explored.

'I suppose I could move away for a short time, say two months.'

Suddenly, to my astonishment, Mrs Young was on her feet. I thought she would be happy at the prospect of a break, but here in action was an example of one of the strangest quirks of domestic violence. She was actually prepared to put up with it, no matter what the effect on her children.

'No, no, no,' she said, 'What am I going to do when he's gone? Who's going to clean the swimming pool?'

There was a hush in the courtroom. Her words hung in the air for several moments, and her selfishness took our breath away.

She realised what she had said, but not before Issie did. It was clear that this woman's first thoughts were of her swimming pool. Clearly, her daughter came second.

Issie bolted out of the courtroom. I don't think Issie would forget those words for the rest of her life: 'Who's going to clean the swimming pool?'

I adjourned the court in disbelief.

That incident left a deep impression on me and I can still see it as though it happened just last week, yet it was over ten years ago. As Issie's mother sat before me that morning, I wondered again how that woman could have remained with her husband. How could she forgive him? Wasn't she terrified of him? Wasn't she too terrified to remain with this man? I don't know if I will ever know the answers to those questions but I surely had a thousand opportunities to try and solve the mystery through days like that one.

I recalled when I began in private practice in Glebe and was appointed by the court as the solicitor for deserted wives who wanted to make applications for maintenance for themselves and their children. In a way it was a thankless task for a solicitor in private practice. Costs were awarded against the husband by the court at the same time as an order was made for him to pay maintenance to his wife and family. Usually the husband disappeared or got back together with his wife and I never was paid. I became very philosophical about it because it was a great teacher of court procedure. I was on my feet in court most of the day, learning to cross-examine witnesses and present evidence. The money not coming in didn't really worry me, at least not until the bills had to be paid.

The first women's refuge in Sydney was 'Elsie's' and it was in Glebe, not far from the court. It was from Elsie's that these deserted wives came, and before Elsie's there had been nowhere for them to go, nowhere for them to hide from the brutality of their husbands. Many of my clients in those days were women who had no family support, no financial backing. They were battlers fleeing the violence in their homes, fleeing with their kids and wanting the beatings to stop. But because it was so hard fending for themselves, most of them went back. Just because it was easier.

Their first hardship was waiting for financial support to come through from the Government, their second was finding proper accommodation. Living with a group of women, all with similar stories, some handling the moment better than others, together with the absence of privacy, overwhelmed them.

Gradually they thought that maybe it wasn't really that bad, or it wasn't as bad as being without a man. Listening to complaining women all day as they sat around smoking and yelling at the children who were missing their dads made them even more depressed.

I cannot remember one exception. Each of those women had come from a childhood filled with some form of violence, be it a drunken father or mother, arguments over money or the lack of it, depressed living conditions and no expectations that life could get better for them. Their low self-esteem convinced them this was their lot in life, as it had been their mother's.

I saw their husbands in court. They saw me as one of those liberated women who put ideas into their wives' heads about their 'rights'. None of their backgrounds were much different from their partner's. They got their sense of power by being lord of the household, where wife and child jumped when spoken to or copped a backhander if they didn't. They all knew who was boss.

So I went through that period from 1970 to 1982 witnessing only the lower socio-economic side of the story, and it wasn't really until I sat on the Bench that I became aware that domestic violence was not restricted by income. There I heard educated women, wealthy women, worldly women, women like Issie's mother, give me the same excuses why they *had* to remain in an intolerable situation.

Issie could so easily have become a street kid. There are many street kids running from situations identical to hers; kids who are unable to go home because they can't tolerate the violence that is there. These are the lost ones who receive no sympathy, especially when they come from an 'intact, two-car' family, attend a good school and have family holidays.

The violence is often so well concealed that people don't bother to inquire why a child with all these benefits would rather rough it on the streets. The child is usually dismissed as a dead loss and one of those to whom you can give everything and it is never enough.

The records and statistics show that the majority of street kids return home eventually. Like the battered women, so many damaged and sad children return home to the environment that drove them out because the alternatives are just too hard.

But back to court. Within a week of Issie there was another case of a youngster fleeing from domestic violence, but in circumstances far different.

I had just resumed after lunch when Snowy was brought in, a fifteen-year-old with hair almost Persil-white. He looked like a little angel and I loved him instantly.

Pamela, the overworked district officer with the Surry Hills area of the Department of Family and Community Services, as it was known then, brought him in. He looked dirty and in need of a long shower.

'We found him,' said Pamela, her eyes hinting humour, 'in a clothing bin. He wasn't alone. He was there with Bruce Lee.'

She winked and I smiled at young Snowy.

'And who, may I ask, is Bruce Lee?' I inquired.

'He's my dog,' he said, and then I realised that I had heard Bruce Lee earlier, barking from outside the court where the district officer had tied him.

'We tried to bring Snowy here by himself, but he wouldn't come without the dog, so we brought them both,' Pamela said.

'Snowy,' I said, 'we have to find you a better sleeping spot.'

'Not if I can't take Bruce Lee with me,' he replied.

I said, 'Fair enough.'

I looked to the district officer sitting at the side of the court and asked her to ring around and see who could take both Snowy and Bruce Lee.

'Not one without the other,' I said.

I stood the matter down for the officer to make her calls and went through a couple more cases. Then the district officer came back into court, shaking her head.

'No joy, I'm afraid, Your Worship. No facility can accommodate a dog,' she said.

I looked at Snowy and winked.

'Keep trying,' I told the officer. 'Look, go through every departmental establishment and then get on to the Sallies or, I know, ring Bill Crews at Exodus. This sounds just the right type of problem for him to tackle.'

I stood Snowy's case down again and called on the next case. Within half an hour Snowy was back in court.

'There is joy this time, Your Worship,' Pamela said.

Bill Crews, who runs the Uniting Church at Ashfield, and is wonderful with young people, could take both Snowy and Bruce Lee for a short time. There was a house at the back of the church run by the Exodus Foundation that provided short-term accommodation for homeless kids.

'What does that mean?' asked Snowy.

'Well, it isn't for a year, okay? Where are your parents? Do you want us to communicate with them? Are you on good or bad terms?' I looked at him. He was emotionless.

'Mate, you would not want to know them,' he said. 'You care more about me than they ever did. They're too bloody busy having a good time to think of anyone else but themselves and apart from that they are always belting me. You can speak to them, but they won't come.'

And Snowy was right. Despite numerous requests and pleas, they refused to attend court. But Snowy knew none of this. I didn't want to put him through any more pain. Of course, I did have the power to make them attend, but it was bad enough that he was correct—they didn't care a fig about him.

It wasn't easy finding permanent accommodation for Snowy. He was either too old or too young, he needed a parent to work through the family problems with him, he was a boy, and on it went. Where I did not want him was in a refuge.

Refuges were never designed nor meant to house young people or children long term. They were built expressly for short-term emergency accommodation. Due to lack of suitable temporary housing, refuges are now used to house young people, not only during a court case which can last for many weeks, but also for varying periods of time until suitable accommodation is found, if ever.

When I adjourned a matter such as Snowy's, one of the orders I always made was that the child be held in a place of safety. How could I ever be satisfied that the place where the child was being held was safe when some refuges weren't secure at night, and other refuges took in any child from quite a young age up to sixteen, maybe seventeen, and you had a traumatised child thrown in with a seasoned teenager who was doing the rounds of the refuges? After being advised that there were refuges that were not staffed at night because the staff worked office hours and the children were left to their own devices in the evening, I made a point of asking to which refuge it was intended to send a child.

Unfortunately, the public has very little insight into the plight of these children who are forced to live away from home. Children don't have a choice. Circumstances are such that it is often unsafe for them to live at home, unsafe emotionally, physically and for their well-being. For some reason, the general public has little patience for such children, and the remarks that are made about them and the tags placed on them are very similar to the remarks and tags worn by Aborigines.

One point of contention is the living away from home allowance and I know that originally this allowance was badly administered. When it was introduced in 1986, it was for young people who could not, would not, or were not allowed to live at home. They received $222.10 a fortnight. In my view, some district officers abused this allowance by recommending it for children who were not entitled to receive it. They were, therefore, able to remain away from a decent home where, with some family counselling and mediation, that child could and should have been living happily. Yet through this intervention, families were split and irreparable damage was done to them. Eventually, because of the hue and cry over this allowance some sense was brought to bear, and these days more inquiries are made to determine whether or not the child is entitled to receive the money.

This allowance caused homeless kids even more trouble, because people thought that the Government was financing them to leave home. The public doesn't seem to realise that quite often these family splits are only temporary, something like a 'time-out' period. Far more kids would go home earlier if proper accommodation were available to them, where the child and their family could be counselled if they agreed.

When I was at the very end of my tether and 'kicking the cat' again about the injustices of this world delivered on the heads of children, the Salvation Army came forward and took Snowy and Bruce Lee to a family on the outskirts of

Sydney. It was a semi-rural area and I could not have asked for anything better for him.

When Snowy came back to court, this time it was with his new family. Snowy and I chatted quite frankly in front of them, and I told him that he had to make a real effort. I knew he had been his own boss for a very long time and it wasn't going to be easy to abide by house rules at first.

I love the honesty and frankness of kids. Snowy stood up, looked me straight in the eye, and said, 'But what if I just don't bloody well like it?'

'Well, you don't run away. You ring me and say you are coming in to see me and we will start again,' I told him.

Snowy never did go home to his real parents and stayed with his new foster family until he was just eighteen.

Jake was another kid I remember well as being a victim of domestic violence, in circumstances more tragic than Snowy's.

While the court was sitting, Debbie and I could both hear if the phone rang in my chambers, and if it did it was generally important. Just before the morning adjournment I heard the familiar ring and Debbie left the court to answer the phone. She was back in a minute looking worried, and whispered to me that it would be a good time to adjourn for morning break. When we got back into my chambers she told me that the phone call had been from the police and they wanted me to go to Camperdown Children's Hospital to identify a child who they didn't think would survive. She said it was Jake.

Jake was only twelve and had been before me a few weeks earlier after receiving a severe beating from his father. His family had been with him in court and it was obvious that his was a very unhappy household indeed. It appeared that the mother, as well as her son, was on the receiving end of regular beatings. She refused to detail them to me, and Jake himself was unwilling to identify what his father had been doing to him and his mother. I couldn't really do much about it except adjourn the case and ask for reports.

The reports showed that Jake had been in Australia with his family for about ten months. The family were Maori and he was the eldest of three boys. It seemed they were pretty happy with their extended family in New Zealand, but getting work had been a big problem for the father and he wanted a decent life for his family. So they decided to come to Sydney where both parents would work hard. Well, at least that was their plan. But they found work wasn't easy to get in Sydney either, and the family ended up having to accept social security, and charity as well, and this was too much for the father to bear. Drinking and depression followed quickly. They had no money to get back to New Zealand and yet the father would somehow find enough money to spend his days in the pub with his mates. When he came home each evening he was full of guilt as well as alcohol and the violence began.

I returned to the Bench and quickly finished up the other few matters remaining, and when I got back to my chambers there were two policemen waiting for me.

'We've been told to drive you to hospital,' said the young constable, who looked like he had been up all night and probably had.

'This Maori bloke belted the shit out of that poor little kid and took off. He's out there somewhere, and we're hoping he'll try to get to the hospital to see his missus and the kid, and then we'll be able to get him.'

As we drove down the Minda driveway and turned into Joseph Street the policeman turned around and looked at me. 'You won't like what you're about to see, Mrs Holborow' he warned.

He wasn't wrong. I walked into the ward where Jake lay in a coma. His mother was beside him, crying and holding his hand. I was horrified to see the unmistakable imprint of a shoe in the middle of Jake's face. His eyes were not visible because of the swelling and it was only by the tips of his eyelashes that you could tell where his eyes were. The beating had knocked his nose off-centre, and his lips were blue. I walked up behind Jake's mother and patted her on the shoulder. She stood up as though she was in court. There was so much pain in her eyes. My arms went round her and I kissed her on the cheek. She was a proud-looking woman, tall and slim, but she herself had bruises on her face and arms.

It turned out that the previous night Dad had come home and started laying into his wife and it all got too much for Jake. In an uncontrollable rage, he took to his father, who retaliated by knocking Jake to the ground and then smashed his foot down into his face with the full force of his 102 kilos. Jake's skull was fractured, a cheekbone was smashed, his teeth knocked out, and the doctors had had to drill into his skull to release the pressure on his brain caused by bruising. His mother had absolutely no friends she could call on, and the only thing the police could find to help them with the family's history were Jake's court documents—hence their calling me.

'Yes, that's him all right,' I said to the policemen. I didn't at that stage quite know what to do, but I told the mother that we'd get some people to help.

As we were leaving the hospital, just as the police predicted, Jake's father was walking towards the emergency department doors. The police left me standing there and bowled up to him, expecting a fight, yet there was none. Instead this big, good-looking man held his head and cried.

When I got back to Minda we sat down to work out what to do. Among the court documents was the address of the next of kin in New Zealand and we spoke to the wife's brother. All their relatives got together, and within a day Jake's maternal grandmother was on a plane to Sydney.

The good news was that Jake did recover. The bad news was that it was now up to me to decide what was going to happen to the boy, and really, to his family. The father had been remanded in custody, but I wanted to see him before I decided on Jake's fate.

The day came for Jake to appear before me again, and I must say that his recovery appeared nothing short of miraculous. The face of the apprehensive little boy sitting in my court was nothing like the lump of raw meat I had seen in hospital, and I was overjoyed. Jake and his mum waited patiently for me to deal with some other cases, and when their case was called the father was brought in from Long Bay Gaol where he was on remand for the beating, escorted by two Corrective Services officers in their blue uniforms. On seeing his father Jake couldn't help himself. He bolted across the court towards him and I thought something terrible would happen. Instead, Jake threw his arms around his father, and his father did the same to his son, and they both started to cry.

I asked the mother what she thought should be done, especially, as seemed likely, the father would spend some time in gaol.

'We just shouldn't have left New Zealand,' she said, 'if we had stayed it would have been all right. We've got family there, he's got lots of friends. This is a real mess. All we want to do is go back and I think it will be okay. He's not a bad man, you can see that, and he loves his children. If he was over there, at home, this wouldn't have happened.'

When I asked the father what he wanted, again he put his head down and cried. I don't think anyone needed to tell me how he felt. Despite his grief and shame, he had a very proud bearing.

I let him cry for a time and then told him, 'I share your tears.'

He looked up at me and I continued.

'What we are going to do today is that now I have heard from your wife, I'm going to hear from you as to how you propose to protect this child from ever having to go through this pain again,' I said.

He broke down again and kept shaking his head.

'Am I right if I said that you would all be better off back with your family in New Zealand?' I said to him.

His gratitude was immediate and incredible.

'Yes, yes, that's what we both want, but I might not be able to, might I?' he said, referring to his upcoming sentencing on the charge of assaulting his son.

'Maybe not yet because it was a terrible assault, but eventually,' I said.

I asked if he wanted his wife and family to stay here if he went to gaol.

'No, I want them to go back as soon as possible,' he said.

It was also my view that the quicker the child was put in the care of the mother and returned to New Zealand, the better.

Unfortunately, it was not in my power to deal with the father's case, that was for another magistrate in an adult court. I could, however, make sure that the file got before the other magistrate, with my views that the whole family would be better off in New Zealand.

The magistrate who the father eventually appeared before made what I think was the right decision. The father had already spent a lot of time in gaol on remand, and was not gaoled further. He was placed on a bond, and one of the conditions was that he return to New Zealand. It had been a terrible period for them in their lives and one I'm sure they determined to put behind them as quickly as possible.

I don't think I will ever be able to rationalise that people can still manage to love those who have inflicted incredible cruelty upon them. It is, however, the strangest thing about the curse of domestic violence. There are, of course, many cases when domestic violence gets absolutely out of control, especially if the perpetrator has access to a gun. But how do you predict which cases, left without any judicial interference, will resolve themselves and be seen as a dark episode in an otherwise good relationship, as opposed to those which will end in the tragedy of maiming and murder? I think I got it right on most occasions. At least I hope I did.

CHAPTER 4

# WHERE THERE'S A WHEEL, THERE'S A WAY

I HAD broken my leg and was stuck in a damned wheelchair. It was one of those silly accidents that should never have happened, but the injury was really quite severe and the road to recovery was via a wheelchair, crutches and then a walking stick. On the night it happened I'd been in such a hurry as usual and had rushed through the front door at home, straight into my adopted son Jacob's bag which he, like most boys, had dropped in the middle of the floor. I found it so frustrating that each day I had to get a taxi to and from Minda Court and wait for someone to wheel me in. I'd never been one for being mollycoddled and it drove me mad!

This morning the taxi had just dropped me off and I was waiting on the pavement for Steve to wheel me in when a car came screeching along and pulled up next to me outside the court. Out jumped Bill, barely old enough to drive, with a few cans of soft drink and a number of packets of chips and Twisties. He was genuinely upset as he came up to me.

'I've only just heard what happened to you,' he said, as he almost threw the food and drinks into my lap.

There was a lump in my throat, and it wasn't in anticipation of the Twisties.

'Oh Bill, this is lovely,' I said, and I meant it.

'You're my family, you know. You are my family,' he said before he turned and ran back to the car, which I suspected was stolen, just as I have little doubt that the food he gave me, while cold, was as hot as the car.

Bill is another example of how the system fails children, children who no-one really cares about. Bill is provided with a Christmas present on Christmas Day by the system, but there's no-one to tuck him in his bed, no-one to kiss him goodnight, no-one to love him. God, the Bills of this world used to break my heart.

Bill had been seven when he first came to court. A blond, skinny little thing with spiky hair and very buck teeth. His dad was Swedish and his mother suffered from schizophrenia. He'd been in foster care and he was moved around to something like twelve placements in six months. There were many reasons for this, mainly because he was very withdrawn and for some reason hated people getting close to him, both physically and emotionally. I think he knew he was a plain-looking child, but if only he had realised it was his plainness that made you want to hold him, reassure him and love him. He wasn't very bright and I don't know how bad his history was before he came to me because we had very few details. His mother was itinerant and couldn't provide for him and he'd been in so many foster places that he found it very difficult to attach to people. Every time he came to court, he appeared bewildered. It didn't appear to matter to him that each stay with each family was so short. In fact, I think he just took it as a fact that life itself was itinerant and isolation from other humans was his lot.

I'd seen him in my court now and again, all to do with welfare matters. It had been hoped his mother would eventually be in a position to care for him, but after twelve months it became obvious she would never be able to manage. She moved out of his life altogether, and Bill became totally reliant on the state for his comfort, welfare and upbringing.

By the time he was thirteen, he was before me for a minor criminal offence. I hadn't seen him for four years, although he had been a regular visitor to my court until he was nine. We had renewed our acquaintance—he recognised me and I recognised him. On that occasion I'd had a quiet word in private with his district officer, who was a very caring young woman.

'For God's sake, can't the Government find enough money to do something with that child's teeth? If that could be done, maybe he would have more self-esteem if he could look in the mirror and smile back at himself, instead of looking in the mirror and seeing a haywire picket fence,' I'd said to her.

Sure enough, this district officer organised a trip to the orthodontist and his teeth were straightened so that now they looked a bit like Humphrey Bogart's, rather attractive, slightly bucked teeth. But still Bill would not stay in one place. Eventually he went from his foster placements in private homes into institutions. Unfortunately, he still attached to nobody. He had slipped into the life of coming and going very much at his own will at whatever institution he happened to be in. It was inevitable that he would be involved in petty crime. His crimes were all pretty minor and I could never find it in my heart to give him a custodial sentence and deprive him of his liberty. We'd have a chat every time he came to court, and it seemed to me that the district officer and I were just about the only people he could relate to. In some odd way we were both authority figures who would never really get too close to him. I felt he had been punished all his life. As he drove off in his car that morning, I knew it wouldn't be the last time I would see him. As it turned out, his once-petty crimes became more serious and it became obvious he would have to be sent inside. I made sure that I wasn't sitting on the Bench on the day of that sentencing.

It was crime day at Minda and the first child before me,

Pete, was no stranger to the court. Notorious for his escapades with stolen cars, this time it looked as if he had learned his lesson the hard way. When Pete came into court, both his arms were in plaster and stuck out at right angles to his body, with his hands resting on two steel rods that were strapped to his waist. His head had a halo of steel around it held there by a rod down his back. He walked like Frankenstein and just looking at him you ached as you could see he was in terrible pain. He'd had a near-fatal crash when the kombi van he had stolen ran out of road and he catapulted through the windscreen. His case was to be heard in another court, but in the meantime he was here before me to make an application for bail. I was aware that at that time we had some young but already 'heavy' criminals in Minda Detention Centre and I feared for this boy's welfare. It looked to me as though if anyone touched the halo or bumped his plaster he would just disintegrate.

I received the medical evidence and I wondered at the skill of surgeons and medical science that this boy had been put together so well. I granted him bail. I had no fears that he would be escaping from home, or would reoffend, or that he would not turn up at court to answer his bail, because he had two months before the plaster would be removed and he would be reviewed by the doctors.

Before he left the court, I wanted to have a talk with him.

'I guess this time you realise you are not invincible. You realise that you can be hurt and you can die if you continue to live in this daredevil fashion,' I said.

He looked at me and simply said, 'I've stolen my last car.'

I thought, fair enough. You couldn't go through that much pain, you couldn't be in the situation he was in without having learned something.

As he left, I unscrewed the jar of jelly beans I always kept on the bench and picked myself a yellow one. On my first day at Minda, when I had walked into court with the jar, the police prosecutor had said to the court constable, 'Oh shit, she's going to give the little buggers a jelly bean to be good.'

He did not tell me this until I had been there for a year, when he thought he knew me well enough and knew I could laugh at myself. He didn't know I was a diabetic.

Glancing through today's four-page list, I saw that Pete was the first of only two SMVs, or stealing motor vehicles as they are correctly known. Coincidentally, the other one, Ted, was also an old 'friend' of the court.

But only two! How different from when I first began to sit at Minda I thought. In about 1982, by far most of the crimes that came before me related to the theft of motor vehicles. It was an epidemic! After a couple of weeks of this, I decided that not only had the public had enough, but so had I. There was no way I was just going to give these kids a lecture and send them back out into the street, because it wasn't doing them or the public any good.

So one Monday morning the very first child who pleaded guilty to stealing a motor vehicle was unwittingly enlisted to help.

'I'm putting you on probation for six months,' I told him, looking stern.

'If in the next six months you come before me and you are found guilty of stealing a motor vehicle then you will spend six months in an institution, and what I propose to do now is this. I cannot commit you to an institution without a full report, and I intend to order that report today so that it is on the file and if you come before me within the next six months, I will be satisfied that I have the relevant report and there will be no delay in your committal.'

Once he had taken that in, I continued.

'And I would recommend to you that you spread the word among your friends that this is what is going to happen at Minda from now on,' I told him.

I don't know whether he thought I was joking or not, but

I know that for the next six months only four re-offenders came before me. In each case, there were no questions asked, they went straight into institutions.

During that time, although there were fresh offences, I gave them all the same talk and within a year the offence of SMV hardly appeared in Minda's list. It was no small satisfaction I felt when I read in the paper twelve months later that the incidence of car theft had dropped dramatically.

I was sure that Minda had played a major role in the statistics and as I sat there waiting for the police prosecutor to call the next matter, I remembered the day I looked down the list and thought there must have been a mistake. I had two children before me listed as uncontrollable. They'd stolen a motor vehicle—but their dates of birth alarmed me. One was seven and one was eight! As soon as they walked into court, one with his mother and the other with his mother and father, I knew that there was no mistake. They were tiny and couldn't possibly have been over seven or eight.

The police sergeant that day had great difficulty in keeping his voice steady and a smile from his lips as he read the facts.

A police car travelling in the opposite direction to the car in which the two 'criminals' were travelling almost ran into a telegraph post, because it appeared to the police as though no-one was driving the car.

The police did a very quick U-turn and pulled up beside the car which was travelling very slowly and saw the eight-year-old squatting in the driver's seat, and on the floor of the car was the seven-year-old who was pushing the accelerator.

It was very difficult to keep a straight face as these would-be car thieves stood before me. Of course had they gone onto a main road, it could very well have been fatal, but fortunately it wasn't, and I thought from the looks on their parents' faces, that they had probably been punished already. The parents were far from laughing or smiling.

Their sons had taken a neighbour's car and the parents told me that by way of apology for what they had done, they had to do jobs appropriate for their age for the neighbour over the next three months.

What the kids didn't know was that I couldn't really do much about them anyway. They weren't ten years old, which is the age of criminality. The complaint of 'being uncontrollable' had been laid by the police under the old *Child Welfare Act*, but was not considered a criminal matter. The kids, however, certainly looked scared enough. I had a gut feeling that from the day of their capture they would have been very controllable. As often was the case, neither of them was doing very well at school. No-one had looked into that aspect, so I ordered some reports to assist the parents whom I thought appeared to be extremely responsible people. It was found that one little fellow was dyslexic and the other had Attention Deficit Disorder, so both could be helped. I never saw them again.

When I'd arrived at Minda, there was an open courtyard with seats on three sides where the church welfare ladies sold cups of tea, coffee and cordial to the parents and their children. Minda consisted of a juvenile detention centre and the court complex. I didn't have much to do with the detention centre itself, apart from supplying it with the young people who made its unfortunate existence necessary. The whole place was dark, dismal and foreboding. The court complex had been built around a bricked-in courtyard and along two of the walls were narrow wooden benches. When it rained the courtyard filled up with water and there was no shelter anywhere. Mums often stood their toddlers on the benches to keep their feet dry.

Opposite the courtroom there was what was called a storeroom, but it took a fair bit of lobbying on my part until someone found a key. When we opened it up, it turned out to be a dumping ground for obsolete departmental files. But at least they were dry! The store room was only small, but we turned it into a waiting room and persuaded the department to furnish it. Some solicitors brought in plants for the courtyard and after more lobbying, we got the courtyard roofed.

There was, however, still no privacy for the children. Some of them were brought in handcuffs from the police station and had to walk through that courtyard. It was as though they were being paraded as an example to the others. It took a year, but finally a small fence was built to stop this public humiliation.

There was a second, small courtroom at Minda which was no longer used as a court. With donations from various charities and $1000 from the New South Wales Law Society, we turned it into a parents' room stocked with disposable nappies, spare feeding bottles and four sets of clothing we could give to a parent for their baby or young child. With all those changes we'd gone a long way to overturning the ingrained attitude that kids who found themselves in trouble, and their parents, were third-class citizens and would be treated as such.

I was only the third magistrate to be appointed to the Bench from private practice as opposed to coming through the public service system. In the public service you just did not lobby for the public. It seemed to me, coming from outside, that you were expected to go to work, do your job and then go home. Innovations, even simple ones, had low priority. Thank goodness that's all changed now, and with magistrates being appointed from the private sector it will never return to those dark days.

Yet the changes we made outside the court still didn't alter the reality of what went on inside the courtroom itself. There were many harrowing and downright frightening moments. One kid threw a microphone at me and after that all microphones were screwed down. Another child picked up a spare typewriter we kept on a table and threw it up at the Bench. It flew just past my head. It must have looked like something out of *Monty Python,* as I kept on talking while I ducked. I certainly wasn't going to give this kid the satisfaction of knowing he had rattled me. What really did rattle me though was brought on by a long-standing phobia I have about rats. One fifteen-year-old arrived in court and I noticed something I couldn't quite make out on his shoulder. But as he walked towards the Bar Table I recognised, to my increasing horror, a large, white, and to me, terrifying rat. I shot into the air above the Bench and ended up with my feet on the seat, such was my panic. I yelled to the prosecutor, 'Get him and his pet out of this courtroom!' The boy was defiant and said, 'He goes everywhere with me.'

I said, 'This is a news flash. Get out!'

The Sergeant could see that I wasn't joking. I said to him, 'I don't care whether you put the boy or the rat in the cells or both the rat and the boy in the cells, but just make sure it doesn't escape.' The kid had his girlfriend outside, and it turned out they carried this creature everywhere with them in a basket with a lid, and that's where the rat spent the rest of the morning.

One of the more tragic stolen motor vehicle cases I'd been involved with was while I was still a practising solicitor and this particular boy was doing his Higher School Certificate. He wasn't brilliant, but he had given his mum and dad much pleasure by remaining at school and striving to get his HSC so that he could go on to get a good job.

The boy's name was Darren and on Christmas Eve he was sitting on the fence outside his house talking to two good mates when a car pulled up. Darren knew the car had to be stolen. He was asked if he'd like to have a drive and he said, 'Yes, around the block.'

It is strange how a set of circumstances can set in train a night of horror, with one error after another. It was a quiet suburb and Darren could see no harm in driving around the block, but he had only gone a very short distance when a highway patrol car came into the street for an entirely different reason, saw the four youths and put the siren on.

The boy who'd stolen the car said, 'God, if I'm caught, they'll lock me up for a year.'

Unfortunately, at that moment Darren's good judgment went out the window. Caught up in the panic, he put his foot down and the car sped away with the police in chase. Darren was a totally inexperienced driver. He got onto a main road, it started to rain, he was coming to an intersection and he couldn't stop. He went through the intersection, lost control of the car, slid into the first car waiting at the lights to cross over the intersection and killed the driver instantly. The driver was a young married man with two very small children. In the car was a Christmas tree, the lights to be strung around the tree and many presents.

I had been the duty solicitor when Darren was brought to court. He pleaded guilty and the magistrate called for the police brief which she would read before she sent him to a higher court, the circumstances being too serious for the Children's Court to deal with.

At this preliminary hearing, the wife of the man Darren had killed came to the court. To this day, I still admire her. She was with her father. She was young, well spoken and in control, but only just. Darren couldn't look at her. His hands shook, his shoulders shook. Although I was never in favour of solicitors, especially female solicitors, putting their arms around their clients or holding their hands during a serious case, I wanted to put my arm around Darren. He was granted bail with strict conditions because he had no prior convictions. As we went to leave the court, I said to him, 'Do you feel up to saying something to her? Is there anything you think you could say that might help her?'

He said, 'I don't know, I don't know what I can say except I didn't mean to kill anyone.'

I said, 'Well just tell her that.'

This was where I admired this boy. There was nothing in his history to prepare him for this, to prepare him for what he'd done. It must have taken a lot of strength. Wearing his Sunday best clothes his mother had dressed him in for court, he walked up to this widow in the foyer of the court. He hung his head and she couldn't look at him.

'Darren would like to speak to you,' I said.

I stood back and left the two of them alone.

He started to cry and said to her, 'I'm sorry, I'm sorry for what I've done, but I didn't mean to kill him.'

She started to cry as well and said, 'I'm sorry too. It is a Christmas I will never forget, but the children are so young that they will forget and I'm sorry for you because I believe you. I wish you good luck.'

This woman had the dignity of Garry and Grace Lynch, Anita Cobby's parents, who went through that whole horrific trial after her murder with such dignity, and yet their pain was no less than that of any other person who has lost a loved one in tragic and avoidable circumstances.

Darren did his HSC from an institution when he got quite a hefty sentence.

But back to that Friday, which had started off with my unexpected breakfast courtesy of Bill.

The rest of the morning passed uneventfully, but during lunch John, my court officer, burst into my chambers and said, 'Ma'am, come and have a look at this.'

He wheeled me to a side window and there was another court regular, Ted, getting out of a white sports car, the flashiest car you can imagine.

I looked at John. 'He wouldn't have stolen it, would he? He wouldn't dare drive to court in it?' I said.

Of course John couldn't help himself, he did an immediate check on the number plates but the car was legal and registered in Ted's name. I couldn't wait for Ted to come into court so I could find out how he came by this car.

Ted used to steal cars on Friday or Saturday nights to get from point A to point B. You wouldn't call him a joy-rider—he had a purpose. He wanted to go somewhere, he stole a car. He wanted to get home, he stole a car. Nothing would stop him and finally he had turned eighteen and was back in court to finish off a matter which he had committed while still a juvenile.

When he came into the courtroom after lunch, Ted strutted. He didn't 'need a solicitor, thank you' and would appear for himself. Of course the truth was that he'd appeared in court as often as some of the more junior solicitors.

I didn't want to admit to Ted that I'd been peeping through windows at him and asked, 'How did you get to court today, Ted?'

'In my car, Barbara,' he said. He always called me Barbara, but there was no disrespect meant. It was a sort of one-upmanship on his part.

'Well, my goodness, what have you got?' I said, feigning surprise.

So he named this car. An MGB I think.

'Ted, however could you afford one of those?' I asked.

In my mind I had Ted with a loan, not being able to keep up with the payments and the car being repossessed or him stealing to make up the payments. I also thought the insurance would have been dud. None of that!

'I had a bit of luck, I won second prize in a lottery,' said Ted.

I said, 'Well done!'

'And I spent the money on my car and the insurance and I don't owe anybody anything,' he continued.

'Well that's great, Ted, and tell me, what are you going to do when another Ted comes along and borrows your car to go out on a date?' I wanted to know.

Without hesitation he said, 'I'll shoot the bastard.'

Ted reminded me of another car-mad kid called Sam. He was a Lebanese boy with a good sense of humour. He knew he couldn't put one over me, but he used to think it was worth a try. Like Ted, he loved cars, even when he was not old enough to legally drive them. At fifteen he would come into court with the most glamorous girls, years older than himself, but then Sam looked nineteen when he was fifteen and had a moustache that most Australian men would envy—if they wanted to grow a moustache. Eventually through good times and bad, Sam had reached eighteen. He'd come back before me instead of an adult court magistrate because, like Ted, he had an outstanding summons. He'd been caught driving without a licence again not long before his eighteenth birthday.

I'd seen him arrive at court as a passenger in a smart red sports car with the latest glamorous girl. They made an unlikely pair at Minda and actually looked like they were on their way to a nightclub.

In court, Sam assured me that although the car was his and was registered in his name (and my conscientious court constable had already done a check) he never drove it. His companion was his permanent girlfriend, the girl his family had chosen for him, he told me. I very much doubted that Sam's family had chosen this girl to be Sam's future wife. She didn't appear to be Muslim to me and I knew Sam's family was deeply religious. So again Sam was playing games with me and once again I fined him and continued his disqualification.

When Sam got to his car that afternoon to leave the court, at first he walked to the driver's side but then changed his mind and got into the passenger seat and gave his girlfriend the keys. She took off with the wheels spinning and in great style. Up the road from Minda was a service station where I got my petrol. That afternoon, soon after Sam had left, I pulled in on my way home, only to see the girlfriend in the passenger seat and Sam just about to drive away. He'd reached the roadway when he turned his head to look for the oncoming traffic and saw me. I smiled and shook my head. He took his hands off the wheel and held them both up as much as to say, 'You've got me.'

But Sam was never one to bear a grudge. I reported the incident, pretty unfair of me, but Sam needed to be kept off the road, he was a dangerous driver. I had reported it to my court constable and of course Sam was picked up. By then, because Sam had turned eighteen he didn't come before me this time. I was so grateful that he pleaded guilty because I would have been embarrassed having to give evidence against him. I think it would have been some time before Sam would have gained his licence because his record was appalling and the local court magistrate in that area was quite tough.

But Ted was definitely the highlight of that day. The rest of this afternoon was taken up with tedious solicitors making tedious comments and I could see we weren't going to finish by 4 p.m. I was sitting in my wheelchair at the Bench and feeling weary at the end of the week.

At about ten to four, two policemen brought into court a seventeen-year-old boy to whom I'd given bail on the Monday.

I stopped the case I was in the middle of and said, 'What's this? Didn't I give you bail on Monday?'

The prosecutor said, 'Ma'am, he's here on a breach of bail. He's breached his bail conditions, four of them.'

I was irritable and cranky.

'That's it, you're in for the weekend,' I said.

Of course I had no right to do this. I had to send him off to wait for a solicitor to appear for him, I had to listen to the reasons why, or if, he had breached his bail. My leg was hurting and I just wanted to be rid of him.

He decided to stand up for himself.

'Could I just say something?' he said.

'Fine, go on, it's your court. It's a children's court. What have you got to say for yourself?' I said.

'Well, it's all right for you,' he said. 'You're a magistrate and you're wealthy. You'll go home tonight, you'll go out to dinner, you're probably going to a party and will have a really good time. I'll be stuck up there, I'm seventeen, they won't let me smoke. I have things to do. I have a party to go to myself tonight and I have a party to go to tomorrow night and I want to take my girlfriend. My girlfriend has told me that if I get stuck inside again, we're through, and I'm pretty keen on her. I don't think it's fair that you're going to lock me up for the weekend just because I didn't do everything *you* told me I had to do and I don't think it's that important what I did anyway.'

When he stopped to draw breath, I interjected, 'Is there anything else you want to say to me?'

He said, 'I just want to say this. It's all right for you, you're a magistrate, you don't know what it's like to be in the position I'm in. I bet you've got a big flash car, I've got nothing.'

I said, 'And anything else you want to add to that?'

He said, 'No.'

I said, 'All right, come down here to the front of the court please. Stand in front of the Bench.'

He walked down and stood in front of me at the Bench.

I said, 'Have a look at what I'm sitting in.'

And he looked at the wheelchair and said, 'Oh fuck, you're a cripple. Oh God, I'm sorry love, don't worry about it. I'll go in.'

And he left the courtroom without another word. In fact, it had been too late in the day for him to obtain legal representation and he spent the night inside. I gave him bail the next morning.

CHAPTER 5

# DOMINOES

THOSE OF us around at the time of the Vietnam War well remember that the political justification for the brutality inflicted upon those poor people was a thing called the Domino Theory. It was held by the politicians of the time that if Vietnam fell to the communists, the rest of Asia would fall as inevitably as dominoes standing side by side. History shows the stupidity of this contention, but there is a perverse irony in all this. The Domino Theory is alive and well in a sociological, not political fashion, and each of us in Australia is paying for the violence and torture that abounded then in South-East Asia and still goes on in some countries there today. The dominoes I'm talking about are not countries—they're kids. The kids who are affected at the end of the line by something they've got no control over occurring at the beginning. I saw the mindless bloodlust of Vietnam and Cambodia in my children's court, personified in little Asian kids appearing before me who were so brutalised by what they had seen and had done to them in their home countries that nothing they saw or did in this country could ever surprise or terrorise them. They had been been immunised by violence and were now immune to it.

As I've mentioned before, the days at Minda Children's Court were divided into crime and care days, and the crime days were then allocated to cases from different police districts. On Wednesdays, the cases from the Fairfield and Cabramatta districts came before me.

Those areas have the biggest ethnic mix anywhere in Australia and over half the population is Asian. A walk down Cabramatta High Street leaves you in no doubt that you are in a part of Asia, and yet the judicial system that has to deal with Asian crime is still the one handed down to us by the British. It is a system that has, I guess, served well in many of the colonies of Britain, and, all in all, it works well here. But I was having to deal with kids who were forced to flee their country and culture and try to make a new life in a foreign land.

What they needed was counselling, support and rehabilitation, not punishment. No wonder many of them had huge problems.

Every Asian child who came before me had been traumatised by the death of a parent or another relative, or by living in a refugee camp or coming to Australia by boat. One boy told me how he had rubbed sump oil over his sister to save her from being raped by pirates, who then wouldn't touch her because she was too dirty. In my opinion, as well as counselling, so many of these children needed proper accommodation for them and their whole family.

I had been appalled when I learned through the children in my court about their living conditions in Australia. These Vietnamese families had been welcomed here by the Australian Government to start a new life after the tragedy and horror of the Vietnam War, and although many families took up the Government's offer, they hardly swamped our resources. Yet we did not manage to house them even adequately, never mind properly.

Half the Asian children who came before me came to court alone. They had no-one in Australia responsible for their well-being. Some children had come alone through refugee camps, while in many other cases their parents couldn't get to this country and had put their children in the hands of someone else, often a total stranger, to get them away and into Australia. But without the bond of family, these new 'relationships' were flimsy at best, and the children were often left to fend for themselves.

As a good example, I noticed over a period of a few months that the same address, a unit in Cabramatta, was being given to the court as the home address of at least a dozen Asian boys who came before me. Something didn't seem quite right. I told the local police about my suspicions, and in a couple of weeks a sergeant got back to me.

He said he'd discovered that the unit had been leased to an Asian man who, as far as police were aware, didn't exist. It was a fictitious name. The officer told me the unit had become known as a haven for 'the Asian criminal youth element,' and missing children had been found there in the past.

They were concerned enough to raid the place and found twenty-seven youths living in the two-bedroomed unit. They used to take it in turns to sleep on a roster system. On the night of the police raid, they found three adult escaped prisoners, two illegal immigrants, and four juveniles wanted for questioning about break-ins in the area. In total, they arrested eight youths and charged them with various offences.

Not one of these juveniles had a parent in Australia, and it had been very difficult to decide what to do with them because they couldn't return to that address. Most of them however, scarpered for Melbourne instead of turning up in court and I didn't see them again.

Because of the difference in cultures and the total lack of paperwork from the original Asian country, it was often easy for a smart youngster to hoodwink poor magistrates like myself. I remember a guy called Ha who played a game with me every time he came before my court.

No-one wants to come before a court, but if you do and you are young it's better to keep away from the adult system as long as possible. Ha was quite often in my court for petty crime such as stealing, minor drug offences and the like. Ha looked young, yet there was something about him that made me think he was much older. But what could I do to prove he was over eighteen? He had no original paperwork from Vietnam and every time I asked him how old he was he would, smirking, hand over a photostat of something resembling a birth certificate showing him to be sixteen. He was getting quite cheeky, and I was getting quite mad. I was wondering what I could do when suddenly a memory from my days as a solicitor struck me. I remembered a policeman had once explained to me that there were two places on the body that you could rely on to indicate a person's age—the jaw and the wrists. He said X-rays of a jaw and wrists would reveal the approximate age of someone and get it right to within one year, or at the most eighteen months. I'd never thought that the time would come when I would be able to put that bit of trivial, but useful, information into practice.

That Wednesday, Ha arrived in court with a solicitor, clutching his piece of identity paper. We made sure there was a Vietnamese interpreter in the court on Wednesdays, and through her I explained that I would be entitled to send Ha to an adult court unless he could prove he was sixteen. By this time I could see that Ha was enjoying his little appearances before me. It was a game of cat and mouse with me being the mouse. He had become cocky and I gambled on this.

I explained to Ha that there was a way he could prove to me he was only sixteen. He was to go to the hospital with the detective who brought him to court and have X-rays taken of his jaw and wrists.

He conferred with his solicitor and in very good English said, 'Why not?'

Ha returned in the afternoon and the detective handed

me a note from the specialist, 'I have reviewed this X-ray and in my opinion the subject is approximately twenty-seven.'

Ha smiled. He knew I'd won this round, but I think he enjoyed the sport of trying to put it over all of us. But I had the last laugh—this time.

'Good luck, Ha,' I said as he was led off to the adult court. I wondered how many other twenty-seven-year-olds I had sent to children's institutions.

Shortly after Ha was led away, two undercover police wearing jeans and T-shirts and looking like anything but police officers, brought in an eleven-year-old boy who looked anything but a criminal. He was charged with possessing and supplying heroin. I stared in disbelief. The boy, Yau, was wearing his school uniform and seemed dazed as he stood before me with a police officer on one side and his solicitor on the other. He was so young that I was concerned they had made a terrible mistake. I wanted to know where his parents were, and I was told they could not be contacted as Yau had told police he didn't know where they worked. I decided to stand the matter down until after lunch to give the duty solicitor plenty of time with the boy, and to give the police an opportunity to make more inquiries about his family.

What on earth would I do with him if we couldn't find a relative, I thought to myself. He was only eleven and I couldn't put him into Minda Remand Centre, not even for a night. Minda generally housed kids from the age of sixteen to eighteen and sometimes beyond. And some of those kids were murderers, some on remand, some awaiting an appeal. They were very tough kids.

I didn't even want to put Yau into Yasmar Remand Centre. Yasmar wasn't as tough and the kids were much younger, but there were no eleven-year-olds there. Even though it was the least threatening of the juvenile detention centres, I still thought it was too much for a child not yet in his teens. I hoped they could find his parents.

After lunch, a fairly unhappy undercover policeman came back into court and explained that they had found Yau's grandmother who didn't speak a word of English and would not come with the police. I didn't feel it fair to go ahead.

'Look, I can't deal with this without a relative here. Is he known?' I asked, meaning was he known to police. Did he have a criminal record?

'No, Your Worship,' said Eric, the prosecutor that day.

The duty solicitor explained that he had been instructed by Yau that he did not want to delay or mislead the court. In fact, he wanted to plead guilty today and have it dealt with right there and then.

'What?' I leant forward in my chair. 'Deal with it today? That does throw a different light on it.'

I turned to one of the police officers with Yau.

'Sergeant, do we know anything about the person who supplied this child with the heroin?'

The police officer looked tired as he said, 'No, Your Worship, he says he has never seen him before and doesn't know his name.'

I was in a real quandary. Our institutions were not equipped for eleven-year-olds. I stood the case down again while I considered my options, but really I didn't have any. I allowed Yau to go home on certain conditions and he was to come back in two weeks.

As the police officers led him from court—and they were to make sure he got home safely by delivering him there themselves—I had a terrible thought. What if the people who supplied the child with this heroin were fully *au fait* with the way our children's courts worked? If so, they would know we did not lock up eleven-year-olds and that once dealt with, he would more than likely receive, at the worst, a bond of good behaviour. This would mean that these suppliers would only 'use' children until the kids were caught and then replace them with other youngsters. What were we to do?

Would we be forced to make an example of one of these children as a warning to others?

Today was showing me that I would be playing a whole new ball game here.

Unfortunately, my fears were right. It has now become standard practice for dealers of heavy drugs in the Cabramatta district to use boys as young as possible to act as go-betweens for them and their customers.

I didn't know it at the time, but Yau was my first contact with the 5T gang. It was Eric who first alerted me to the fact that I'd probably already had a few 5T members before me without knowing. He told me to look at their knuckles for tattoos, and when I started doing this it become clear just how strong the gang's grip was over the young Asian community. There were a number of Vietnamese gangs, but by far the most powerful and highly organised was the 5T. It was, however, so confined to the Vietnamese community that very little was known about it in the early 1980s. What we did know was that there was a ladder of progression to the hierachy of the 5Ts, and each step was marked by a tattoo on each of their five knuckles.

One day I learnt what the tattoos represented when I had a young 5T gangster before me on an assault charge, and I was thinking seriously about sending him to a detention centre. I saw Eric furiously shaking his head, to such a degree that I thought I had better find out what was up. So I adjourned and somewhat angrily motioned Eric to come to my chambers straightaway.

When he arrived a couple of seconds later I glared at him. 'What in heaven's name was that little performance about Eric?' I asked.

'Look Ma'am, I'm really sorry. I've never done anything like that before, but I felt I just had to stop you until I could tell you something.'

I was intrigued. 'Okay, well go on,' I said.

Then he explained it all to me and it hit me like a shockwave. Eric told me what each T tattoo represented. The first T was obtained for having sex; the second was obtained for robbery; the third for being convicted of an offence; the fourth for going to gaol and the fifth for murder. In Vietnamese, the slang for each of these acts begins with a T.

It struck both Eric and me that we had unwittingly been responsible for some gang members earning at least two of those Ts. Over the coming year we worked out a strategy to deal with this unusual dilemma. Whenever I'd get 5T members before me, I'd look very closely at their criminal record. If they'd already been committed to an institution and their new crime warranted it, I sentenced them to custody again. But if it seemed that they'd just committed a crime to earn another T, I'd try everything I could to impose a non-custodial sentence, such as a community service order or probation. There were, of course, occasions where I had no alternative but to award them a T.

Perhaps the reason gangs are so attractive to Vietnamese kids is that they represent authority and discipline. The authority and discipline they crave for but don't get at home because, even if they've got parents, they just haven't got spare time for their children because they are usually holding down at least two jobs.

I remember well a decent man called Mr Nguyen who, to me, represented the nub of the problem. His son was in court for stealing and Mr Nguyen took time off work to come to court. The interpreter explained that Mr Nguyen was very sorry for the trouble his son had caused everyone. As this was being explained, Mr Nguyen looked at me and I could feel his frustration and grief. But he was trapped by circumstances and culture. The interpreter told me that Mr Nguyen would have liked me to send his son somewhere he could be taught proper ways and then return home improved. It took a bit of time to explain to Mr Nguyen that

I really couldn't carry out his wishes (even though the thought was very attractive).

I explained I would like to obtain reports and see how we could help the family. When I told him that appointments would be made for the whole family to attend an interview, Mr Nguyen quickly explained to me he could not take more time off work and neither could his wife. We would have to look after his son some other way. I adjourned the matter and left it to the office staff to battle it out with Mr Nguyen, who it seemed had two or maybe three jobs.

Mr Nguyen really represented almost every Vietnamese parent I saw. I wondered when Vietnamese adults slept because they sure worked hard.

Mr Nguyen's son had broken into a house by smashing a window and had stolen jewellery and money. It was an all-too-common offence with the Asian children who came before me. Their favourite time to do it was after school and before their parents got home. The children tended to be very slight and could often climb through the smallest windows left open by people who thought that no-one could possibly fit through the space. Usually they acted alone or, at the most, with a couple of friends. I sent Mr Nguyen's son home with him, knowing he would be back.

Another case also remarkable in crystallising why I was seeing so many Asian kids in trouble involved a Cambodian boy with the anglicised name of Andrew. I'd seen him quite a few times before. He'd had a lot of family problems and was now living in a refuge. Eric read out the facts:

'The young person is charged over the stabbing of one of the boys in the refuge. He had become enraged over missing his turn at the pool table, got a knife from the kitchen and stabbed the boy who had taken his place.

'He made no attempt to run away. He just walked into the garden which was where the police found him, stabbing the ground with the knife.

'When the police asked him what he was doing, his reply was, "I'm getting rid of the blood".'

After Eric read out the charge of attempted murder in court, Andrew dropped his head to one side as he looked up at me and said, 'Yeah, so what?'

What is so difficult for us to understand is that kids like Andrew had seen so much violence in their young lives that it had little effect on them, either witnessing it or using it themselves. Andrew stood before me totally unmoved, yet the boy he stabbed was in hospital critically ill. His victim was to recover, although it looked unlikely at the time.

I thought that Andrew had felt so unloved and rejected that he was bankrupt of emotion. As well as becoming a victim of the regime in his native Cambodia, he had become a victim of the abhorrent trade in babies that had gone on.

At the time, people had watched television programs about the plight of these Vietnamese and Cambodian orphans with these beautiful babies and toddlers looking at the camera with their wide eyes and thought how cute they looked. There had been a lot of advertising for families to adopt these children, which I had thought was hideous at the time. It had made my stomach turn because it was as though they were applying to the RSPCA for an abandoned puppy. Emotion overcame logic.

Nowadays we are far more aware of the cultural problems of intercountry adoptions, but how many young lives like Andrew's have been sacrificed to give us that knowledge?

Most of the children had been incredibly traumatised, yet the well-intentioned adoptive parents tended to take the view that a bit of tender loving care would overcome all that. Some of them didn't attempt to retain their kids' culture but tried to bring them up as dinky-di Aussies, usually giving them non-Asian names. The children weren't encouraged to mix with their own people and their new parents knew little about their culture, and even less about their personal background. Full stop. Yet the children still had their inbred and deeply-rooted cultural needs—and the biggest need of all was to have adoptive parents who understood that.

As if all those problems were not enough, life dictates that they often lose their appealing baby cuteness as they get older and in many cases adoptive parents had not taken these possible changes into account. I didn't know of any girls who were abandoned, but I saw many of these poor boys who were abandoned by their adoptive parents when they reached the age of twelve or fourteen and had physically changed so much.

Andrew was one of those unfortunate boys. He had been adopted by an Australian family when he was a toddler and nobody had attempted to trace his real parents back in Cambodia. I felt the Cambodian children had seen more violence than any other Asian race, which didn't help their plight.

Andrew could be termed a plain-looking boy and without relatives or close friends for support, he had little going for him at the moment. He had ended up in a refuge at the age of eleven when the relationship with his adoptive parents broke down and the authorities had been unable to find foster parents willing to take him. It is a cruel fact of life that unless the children, girls as well as boys, are physically attractive, it is so much more difficult to find them foster homes.

Now Andrew stood before me apparently emotionless. He was totally alone, his Australian parents having washed their hands of him and refusing to come to court. His charges were too serious for me to deal with, so I had to remand him to a higher court. They wouldn't have him back at the refuge, and as there was nowhere else for him to go I had to refuse bail and he went to a juvenile institution until his case could be heard. As he was led away, he looked at no-one. He kept his sad eyes straight ahead. Perhaps his blood parents, if still alive in Cambodia, had thought he was coming to Australia to make a new life free of war and danger. Instead children like him were running amok with violence, triads and gangs. I thought the situation was pretty bad in those days. Just look at it now.

You've probably wondered why I've only referred to boys so far in this chapter. Well, I wondered myself why it was that I never saw Vietnamese or Cambodian girls before me on criminal days. In fact, I had not had one appear before me at that time, which was an interesting issue and I thought somebody should do a study on it.

Of course that changed, and a few years later Asian girls did begin to appear in court, usually for shoplifting but rarely for drugs and not nearly in equal numbers as boys.

I wondered if the parents kept tabs on their daughters more than on their sons or if the girls were not as streetwise. I didn't know the answer and I still don't. Nor did I ever have a Japanese child before me and I only had to deal with one Chinese child. They were such different cultures.

I tended to be very lenient with all these children and I wasn't the only one who was. I think all my fellow magistrates felt the same, and that back in the 1980s it was the right and proper attitude to have. We knew where these children had been and what they had come through with or without their parents, and we wanted to support them and help them lead a better life in Australia. For years there were no means of support for these Vietnamese and Cambodian families. They were lonely parents who were isolated because of their lack of language and because of their lack of understanding of our culture. They needed their own people to help them through this time and while the Government should have provided this, they didn't. The Catholic Church did, however, work with these families and I was able to seek their assistance on more than one occasion. I became very interested in the welfare of South-East Asian children and was proud to be invited to be the patron of Nguan Song Group Homes, a Catholic charity which provides accommodation for Indo-Chinese students.

When the nationalities became more established, it was the Vietnamese people themselves who, recognising their people's needs for such support, rallied and had meetings to help their own community as much as they were able. Out of this came some very caring social workers who made the work of my court much easier.

But even they weren't always able to cope. There was a Cambodian girl called Annie who had studied social work and was devoting her life to helping younger children with similar backgrounds.

Annie was supervising the care of a boy called Tai, and on this day she and Tai were due to appear before me as the last case on the list. Annie walked into court alone, looking very downhearted and without her young charge. Tai wasn't anywhere to be seen.

Tai was only nine, but he was totally out of control. He had the most beautiful smile but behind it he lied, he cheated, he stole, he truanted and his mother just could not do anything with him. She was a widow and she and her son lived with her brother-in-law and his family. The uncle was very hard on Tai, but it was his way of dealing with this wayward child.

Because of Tai's age I really didn't know what we could do. He was still one year under the age of criminality so he could not be charged with any of his offences, which was why he had come before me as a care case. Annie was also doing her best for him. She was well meaning, kind, with a lovely sense of humour, and she cared very much for her people.

The last time I had seen Tai had been just before Christmas and Annie had stood in court and said, 'Ma'am, if it pleases you I have arranged for him to spend Christmas with the Buddhist monks.'

Immediately to my mind came an image of Tai in saffron robes going around Cabramatta with a wooden bowl. Knowing Tai, I didn't think he would be handing over the money he received to the monastery. He would be going to the nearest game parlour and putting it in the machines. But I had kept the smile off my face and said I wished her luck and I hoped that he would remain with the Buddhists.

'Does this mean he will have to have his head shaved?' I asked her.

Her belief in this child touched me because I had become so cynical. I could see no solution. She had, however, patted him on the head.

'We'll see, we'll see,' she had said. I had adjourned the matter until the last week in January, which was going to be a couple of days before Tai went back to school. As they walked out of the courtroom with her arm around his shoulder, everyone at the Bar Table was shaking their heads. They had all at some stage appeared for this child and they were saying things like, 'Oh dear, she's going to be so hurt.'

'I wonder how long he'll last.'

'They'll have to put a ball and chain around his ankles.'

I had thought about Tai during the school holidays and wondered how he was going. But Annie had gone on holidays and I had to wait until the adjourned date to find out how young Tai was faring—which I was about to discover right now.

Annie was very apologetic. She said Tai could not come to court and she felt responsible and bore some guilt that he wasn't with her. There was no way that I could have hurt her feelings by telling her I never thought he would make it, because I knew that she had truly believed he would.

'How long did Tai last at the monastery?' I asked as gently as I could.

With downcast eyes Annie said, 'Four hours.'

'Well, he wouldn't have changed clothes or even had a meal with them, then,' I said.

'I'm afraid not, Your Worship, and we haven't seen him since,' she said.

'What do you mean, has something happened to him? Do you know where he's gone?' I asked.

'No, his mother had disappeared as well,' she said.

'Do you think they've gone together?' I wanted to know.

'I don't know, I'm making inquiries, I only got back from my holidays yesterday,' she said.

'Fine, all right,' I replied and she went off to make some inquiries and find out where they had gone.

I was to learn that Tai and his mother moved to Melbourne. At least I didn't have to worry about him anymore, and it was not my role to inform Melbourne that they had a delinquent nine-year-old Buddhist on their hands—that was up to the appropriate department.

But Tai left me with a wonderful image of this cherub-faced minx in saffron robes with a shaved head and wooden bowl, and I just didn't think that was the type of life that he had mapped out for himself.

CHAPTER 6

# 'I'LL JUST BE TWO MINUTES, OKAY?'

HIS NAME was Storm. He was all of three years old and he looked at me with his big, blue lagoon-sparkling eyes; the eyes of an intelligent and questioning child.

I had begun my court in the usual way, with all the paperwork in front of me. I had already had one experience with Storm.

'You've got a beauty there, Mrs Holborow,' said Terry, the court assistant, while we were discussing the cases of the day in my chambers beforehand. It was 9.30 a.m. and while I didn't always want to know the fine detail of my upcoming cases, Terry always warned me if there was something special. After a couple of years, he knew me well now. We'd been through lots of things, but the theme that kept recurring was how my life—indeed how the juvenile justice system's life—was increasingly being ruled by one thing: illegal, and sometimes legal, drugs.

'You're gunna have a problem with Storm again,' he said.

'Thanks,' I said, 'I need that.' I was joking, but for some reason I didn't ask him why he had singled out Storm. Life was pretty good for me. I was a magistrate and happy with my lot. But being happy about my own life didn't make me any less receptive to the fact that, every day, just outside my door, was a world of seething, juvenile difficulty. For some professionals, when they fix a problem, they can see the results immediately. My role in life was somewhat less defined, but I had no difficulty in knowing that my job was to go to work every day and try to fix up problem kids. But often I would never see the results of my efforts.

'All rise.' And I walked out to another day at work.

One of the carers brought Storm in to the court through a door on my left. I remembered when I had first met Storm, just two weeks beforehand. He had been handed over to the police by the commissionaire of David Jones department store in Elizabeth Street in the city. The commissionaire had reported that a young woman had brought the boy up to him and asked, 'Could you keep an eye on him ... I'll just be two minutes, okay?' And it being David Jones, where the customers have first priority, the commissionaire agreed. When the woman didn't return after two hours, the commissionaire called the police who took Storm away. Storm came before me and was put into foster care and I adjourned the case for two weeks while inquiries were made about his mother. The police got nowhere. But now the case of Storm was before me again.

'Hello, Storm,' I said as this bright-faced little urchin strode confidently through the door, 'do you want to come around here and say hello?'

He looked at me casually. He paused. He stared. He said, simply, 'Get stuffed.' I paused. I stared. I said, simply, 'Oh, very well, Storm.'

Then I told him about some toys I had under my bench and invited him to come around and select one. That seemed to interest him. He climbed up the little platform and looked at the stuffed hippos, panthers and tigers. These toys were kept handy to provide a bit of comfort not only for young kids in the foreign world of a courtroom, but to take home with them. They had been given to us by the Salvation Army, who had in turn received them from some unlikely but exceedingly kind benefactors—a bikie gang who had taken up a collection.

Storm chose two toys and, as he walked back, glanced at a young woman in blue denim jeans and a scraggy black top who had dozed off on the wooden bench behind the Bar Table. He stopped in front of her and then walked on another three metres to an empty chair, despite the fact he could have sat next to her. The sleeping woman was his mother.

Everyone watched this performance in silence, and I couldn't help thinking that Storm was one of the pluckiest little kids I had seen. Not yet three years old, and with people whom he hardly knew, yet he was supremely confident with us. He really had such presence, and was very much his own person who had set his agenda with 'get stuffed'. A hard kid in a hard world.

My attention focused on the sleeper. Jennifer was her name. A classic junkie, feeding her habit through prostitution, but somewhere along the way Storm had come along. Even during this hearing, which would be to decide whether or not Storm should stay with her, Jennifer was in the netherworld of narcotics—her mind ebbing and flowing between reality and fairyfloss. She kept dozing off and it was only when her chin hit her chest that the discomfort of her neck roused her, only momentarily, and away she went again.

Adrian was the department's legal representative for that day.

'Ma'am,' he said, 'as you know, young Storm was left some two weeks ago at David Jones, with the mother saying, "I'll just be two minutes, okay?" Extensive inquiries had failed to identify the mother, that was until yesterday.

'Your Worship might not believe this, but just yesterday Storm's mother, who is currently in court, approached the commissionaire at David Jones and said, "Do you know where Storm is? I left him with you."

'The commissionaire, who could hardly believe his ears, said, "That was two weeks ago and I left him with the police." The police were then called to the store and the mother is currently before Your Worship.

'But I feel that we have no alternative than to apply to have the boy made a ward of the state and for him to go into long-term foster care.'

Clearly it was time for young Storm to leave the courtroom. I indicated to his carer to take him outside and as he left I said, with as big a smile as I could manage, 'Bye bye Storm.'

He turned and said, 'I'll just be two minutes, okay?' Once again no-one spoke. A number of throats were cleared and feet shuffled, but little Storm had once again made his point. The significance of this remark became clear. Obviously it was the way his mother said goodbye to Storm every night as she left to go to work as a prostitute. This was, in turn, how Storm said goodbye to everyone.

Adrian turned again to his notes:

'It is obvious that the mother is totally incapable of looking after him. She has been to various courts for both drug addiction and prostitution. The boy appears to have been brought up in a world of being taken care of by uncles or aunts in seedy private hotels, or being cared for in rehabilitation centres.

'Every indication is that he is very intelligent. Medically, he appears fine, which is probably due more to his ability of being able to take care of himself, rather than being given the maternal care he deserves at that age. I ask Your Worship to study the reports.'

'I'll adjourn the court for twenty minutes while I read the file,' I said and I gathered up the green folder chronicling the short but immensely sad life of Storm and Jennifer.

As I was leaving the Bench, I noticed Jennifer had rallied from her stupor and had tapped her solicitor on the shoulder. He was a nice young man from Legal Aid who would do his best to keep the junkie and her son together. I heard her say, 'I want my baby back. He's mine.'

I sipped my tea while I thought through the case. Neither the fact that Jennifer was a prostitute nor a drug addict were in themselves reasons to deprive her of her child. As a solicitor as well as a magistrate I had been involved with a number of prostitutes who had wanted to keep their children and were able to. They had formed cooperatives and were able to make arrangements regarding working times and child care and were able to carry on their careers. Being a drug addict made life somewhat more difficult in that, parents who are addicts often live in a Jekyll and Hyde world. One minute they're loving and caring, the next they're so out of it they don't know what's going on, and a child can be at terrible risk of both short and long-term neglect. Worse still, in some cases a change in behaviour can make them violent and unpredictable and put a child at risk of immediate and violent physical assault.

And while I was thinking about what to do about Storm, I thought about how drugs had changed my world, and how I had seen some things that I really wish I hadn't. Day after day I saw the effect drugs had on people—from babies only moments old through to people like Storm, teenagers and everyone involved with them.

It always seemed to be late on a Friday afternoon when a young person would be brought to me badly affected by drugs. These poor, rag-doll-like kids, who stole or mugged or schemed to pay for their addiction would be confronted by the spectre of a court and suddenly see a desperate chance for help that they couldn't get in their normal world. I've lost count of the times kids would cry out to me and say, 'Please help me or I know I'll die.' And I knew they were right. Yet there was no magic button I could push whereby a door to a detoxification unit would suddenly open to these young people, especially on weekends if I couldn't find anywhere to send them. Then 'lock 'em up or send 'em back to the streets' were the black or white alternatives. The detoxification units were often so overloaded that I would have to deal with what is basically a medical problem in a strictly judicial sense and send a kid to an institution. I knew it was unfair on the kid, who needed supervision and counselling. It was also unfair to the staff of the institution, who were mainly there to stop the inmates getting out.

What is worse is how drugs, and the pursuit of them, can destroy a family. Such a case was Pete's. In my first week on the Bench he had come before me in very unusual circumstances. Pete was from a very good family, an only child, good at sport and popular at school. He was seventeen when he came into court on a rainy afternoon, his long, blond hair still wet, his strong features altered, so very slightly, by a characteristic darkness under his eyes, and his eyes also a little brighter than they should have been. He had started on drugs the usual way—first a tab of speed, then a few more, then a habit and then his supplier, a former pupil of the same school, had him where he wanted him. First a taste of heroin, one shot taken intravenously, then another. The dragon, having been chased, had finally hooked him. His parents were initially unaware of anything wrong, but when money started to disappear, when all-night stayouts and long, groggy lay-ins in the morning became the norm, then the parents became suspicious. When a mate, a true mate, told the parents, 'I shouldn't be telling you this, but Pete's been taking heroin,' their worst fears were confirmed. But what to do? Promises were broken within hours. Rationale became impossible. But Pete's parents, Ivor and Jan, had one love of their life, their only son, and they could see him being taken away by a dragon they had no knowledge of and didn't know how to fight. Doctors and counselling didn't work with this boy—he had developed a cunning. His parents desperately didn't want to get the police involved, knowing that it would be the last straw for their son, but they wanted him to be forced into changing. So Ivor spoke to his solicitor, who told him that there was a provision in the *Child Welfare Act* by which they could bring him before a Children's Court magistrate without any charges being involved.

So there they were, the three of them, standing before me, each saying they needed help, and what could I do?

Odyssey House was the largest and most effective rehabilitation centre around.

'Do you want to go to Odyssey?' I asked the boy.

'No, I want to stay with my parents,' he said, and he did. They had been, they still were, very close.

'What do you want?' I asked Ivor.

'I want my son back,' he said

'I know, but how do you think I can achieve that?' I asked.

'I don't know; we are desperate.'

This was one of the nastiest faces of our illegal drug problem. It wasn't happening in the gore-and garbage-laden back alleys of Kings Cross. It was happening to a nice and decent family who just wanted it to go away and didn't know how.

The only thing I could do was to somehow try to spark a neurone of discipline and decency that still might reside somewhere in the tortured brain of that boy.

I made very formal orders—'binding and worthwhile orders'. He promised to stay drug free and would accept counselling. They were to report to a district office and make contact with a district officer who would offer as much help as possible. Promises were made and the three of them left court, with a desperate and ultimately futile conviction that these orders, having been given judicial weight, would be obeyed. Within five days Pete was back. I don't think his mother and father had slept during that time. He was on heroin within hours of having left the court, and they had brought him back. This time Pete was frightened by his own behaviour and lack of control. He wept and sobbed and could hardly speak.

'Lock me up, lock me up,' he cried. 'Please just lock me up. I can't do anything about this.'

'What about a rehab centre?' I suggested.

'I know about those places,' he said. 'They're full of people like me and if they want drugs they can get them. You've just got to lock me up in gaol.'

The father started to cry as well. 'He is killing his mother and I'm not far behind,' he said, and he was serious.

I looked at the boy. 'I can't lock you up, because you are not charged with committing a crime, but I need to put you somewhere secure because this is obviously beyond the three of you.'

We got a court officer to ring around the rehabilitation centres, but legally I still could not compel him to go, and he still refused to go voluntarily. He wanted, in a last attempt to cure himself, to be out of the society which had caused him so much temptation and his beloved family so much pain. It was a last-ditch attempt by a basically decent boy to cure himself. If I could have asked him to throw a courtroom chair across the room so that I could have locked him up, I would have done so.

The father solved the problem. Then and there he reported his son to the police, and the police called at the house and, sure enough, found a few caps of heroin that no attempt had been made to conceal.

Pete got what he wanted—a term in an institution, and the parents told me that as soon as he got out after three months they planned to go interstate to get him away from his supplier. They'd rented their house, the father had quit his job, and the three of them would go.

Good luck to them I thought; but how do you ever tell a father that you have no doubt that wherever he moves his son, if he wants to, he will seek out a pusher?

Storm was a boy harmed by his mother's addiction; Ivor and Jan were harmed by their son's habit. One of the saddest sights I have seen in court, however, is the horror of two addicted parents with an addicted child, or children. Yet some of these stories do have a happy ending.

Hugh and Kylie were very young when they discovered the world of drugs. They lived on welfare and petty crime to pay for their addiction, and when they were in their early twenties they had Harry. They received welfare for the baby, but the money went on drugs and someone reported the situation to the Child Welfare Department. Before his first birthday, Harry had made the first of many court appearances, along with his parents. Harry was obviously malnourished, but then again so were Hugh and Kylie. Hugh didn't seem a bad sort of bloke, but Kylie was obviously a whinger.

'How did your baby get in this state?' I asked them.

'Well, we have a habit,' said Hugh. 'I'm sorry, but that's the way it is. I'd like not to have it but I have. We're going to go through rehab.'

'And our cheque was late, and I didn't have enough money for food,' Kylie broke in.

We had a long talk. It seemed Kylie had made a half-hearted attempt at mothering Harry, but it also seemed to me she was far more unstable than Hugh, and Hugh just didn't know how to get away.

'It's decision-making time,' I said 'Harry is going into care. But you will have unlimited access to him, provided you are drug free when you visit. Harry is only seven months old and it is imperative that this thin bond you have with him continue. But you can look after yourselves. He can't, and my first concern must be with him. I don't like taking babies away from their parents, but you must realise that I am doing it for him.'

They looked crestfallen, but I had a feeling that Hugh was very much relieved.

'I will do everything I can to have Harry returned to your care,' I continued, 'but you must come back to me and have a plan for the future. A plan guaranteeing a better life for Harry and also making a better life for yourselves.'

They kissed their child goodbye and handed him over to the welfare officer, and left the court arm in arm. A sad day.

But two weeks later they were back, and not much had changed. They thought they would approach Odyssey to try to fight their addiction, but hadn't got round to it. It was too early to make a decision, to have any plans, they told me. Another two weeks they were back—still no decision, no plan. Another two weeks the same, but this time I was firm. 'I'm adjourning this matter for seven days. You both or either one of you find a rehab and be in it, or I'll be calling for reports to make Harry a ward of the state. You two would do well to listen. I am very, very serious,' I told them.

Next time Hugh turned up without Kylie, but with his mother and a representative of Odyssey House. His mother was not a young woman, and she was very realistic about her ability to care for a young baby with both parents drug dependent.

I guessed Hugh and Kylie had worn out their welcome some time ago and Hugh's mother just didn't want to go down that path again.

In front of me, she said to Hugh, 'I'll help with the baby if you go into rehab and stay clean for three months. But I won't have you and Kylie living in my house with needles and things.'

As Kylie hadn't bothered to turn up, I couldn't get any undertakings from her. Hugh went into rehab after a very short time in detox and during that time his mother visited little Harry in care, and got to know and love her grandson.

Hugh, Kylie, Harry and his grandmother all turned up at the next appearance. Hugh's attitude to Kylie was completely different. He had made an attempt and was drug free. Kylie hadn't done anything and was blaming everyone else for her problems, and it was obvious that Hugh was beginning to realise that she just didn't have what it took to break away from the drug scene. Kylie whined about how sick she had been, that she was living in a refuge but was going to be kicked out 'just' because she came home after curfew and someone had found a needle in her room.

They were drifting apart.

At last the time came for me to make a final order. Another two months had elapsed and this time there were three happy people in court. Kylie had disappeared from the scene. Harry was urecognisable. He was chubby, happy and very secure gurgling away on his father's lap with his doting granny beside him. Hugh looked physically well, and with counselling was working through problems he hadn't realised were behind his drug addiction.

'My mum's going to take Harry and me in and I've enrolled at TAFE,' Hugh said, looking mighty proud of himself, 'and Kylie doesn't want to know about us. She's gone.'

I made a final order that Harry be returned to Hugh's care until he attained the age of sixteen—provided Hugh remained drug free.

The three looked at one another and Hugh hugged his mum. Harry roared approval and the whole court felt like applauding. I felt great as they left. You lose a lot. You win some. And that's what makes it all worthwhile.

There was, however, a great loss that still plays on me today.

Little Sax had been born with withdrawal symptoms. Both his mother and father were heroin addicts. His older brother, Dylan, had already been before me through his parents' drug abuse, and because of the circumstances it was automatic that Sax's case would come before the courts.

It had been Dylan's school that brought his case to the attention of the authorities. He had been turning up wearing grubby clothes, hungry, having had no breakfast and without a packed lunch. The school became concerned and asked his parents to come and see them. They had turned up in a drugged state to see the headmaster. The mother was quite incoherent and barely able to stay awake during the meeting and the father was abusive. The school contacted the Department of Family and Community Services and Dylan came to court with his family as a case of neglect.

I'd let Dylan go home with his parents because he was a plucky little boy and a survivor. His aunt lived nearby and every day after work she used to see him pass her house on his way home from school. He also knew he could phone her whenever he needed help. I'd met his aunt in court and had been impressed with her. The two sisters could not have been more unlike each other. The aunt was married with a teenage child and she used to look after Dylan at weekends. I had made sure that the aunt visited Dylan every evening as a safeguard. It had seemed to work well and Dylan appeared better cared for.

When brother Sax was born, as so often happens in these cases, he stayed behind in hospital when his mother went home. This was not only because of his withdrawal symptoms, but it was also to allow his future to be decided. Why did I let him go home? I have asked myself that question thousands of times and I have no real answer except that listening to his mother's distress in court, listening to her pleas and her promises, I was swayed. I never trusted the father, but the solicitor for the parents, the solicitor representing the interests of Sax and the psychologist who had done a report for the court, all recommended that the baby go home. Dylan had also wanted his baby brother to be at home with them. The last chapter of the story emerged when the parents, the aunt and Dylan came into court on the Monday afternoon, just four days after the baby had gone home.

In tears, they told me that the previous Friday afternoon, when the aunt hadn't seen Dylan going home from school, she went to her sister's house to check everything was fine. She knocked on the door and Dylan had answered.

'Can I come and sleep at your place tonight?' he asked her.

When she asked why, he replied, 'I can't wake anybody up.'

The aunt shouted to her sister and walked into the bedroom as her sister was getting out of bed. Dylan's mother was very angry and asked what she was doing there. The aunt said she didn't think Dylan had been to school and her sister said, 'So fucking what?'

The aunt asked her if baby Sax was all right and his mother said, 'Of course he is.'

The aunt asked to see the baby and when his mother went into the other bedroom to pick him out of the cot, she screamed. The baby was dead, just a day after he'd gone home. It was eventually put down to sudden infant death syndrome, or cot death, but that did not make me feel any better about it.

Poor Dylan had no idea of the impact of what had happened. He was just puzzled. I had to do something for him and it was agreed that he would go and live with his aunt. That must have been the best solution because it was the last I heard of the case.

But back to young Storm. I read and reread the reports. There had been plenty of times in the past when Jennifer had been given the chance to change her ways. I came to the realisation that, without some very forceful persuasion, I had no option but to take Storm away from Jennifer.

Back on the Bench again and the young solicitor tried to put Jennifer's case, but there was really no case. She sat directly behind him, drifting in and out of her own little world.

She still seemed uncomprehending when I said, 'This is a very sad case because Storm is such a wonderful little man, but I am going to have to make him a ward. He will go into foster care.'

She snatched up her bag and drifted from the room, her solicitor following to try to explain the significance of the decision to her.

I knew the sorry saga would not end there. Jennifer had the right to come back time and time again to reclaim her son. I knew she would lead evidence of a dramatic turnaround in her lifestyle. I knew there would be promises of rehab and being a caring mother and all that. What I also knew is that young Storm would probably be with a loving foster family and would probably not see his mother for years. And when, and if, she did convince a magistrate that she had rehabilitated herself, rightly or wrongly, Storm would be uprooted from the family who had helped him through a difficult time and thrust back with the woman who had got him into the mess in the first place. And the foster family who loved him would also be shattered. Every child has a claim to a stable life, but what about Storm? Because of what drugs have done to him, he has very little chance of one. It's my opinion that drug-addicted and unsuitable parents should not be permitted time and time again to apply to get their children back. They say they need time to 'get their act together', but if they haven't done that before a child is born, then maybe they should be given twelve months maximum before the child is placed somewhere permanently.

Otherwise children become pawns in a cruel game played by adults. In those days, heroin was undoubtedly the cause of more crime than any other drug—and it still is. You read a lot these days about so-called 'designer' drugs like ecstasy. But they weren't really a big problem until recently. I didn't see much of them. But they are in addition to, not a replacement for, heroin. I know that the unquenchable desire by a junkie to get money to buy a fix is the cause of a lot of crime. I know that a lot of people want to legalise heroin. But I haven't come far enough to support the legalisation of drugs. My commonsense tells me that you would get rid of the pushers and a lot of crime, but the reality is that when they have tried these sorts of experiments overseas, it hasn't been the panacea that everyone is looking for. Someone once said, 'One of the most pleasant things in life is doing what you're not supposed to do.' I'm sure that those with the desperate and addictive personalities to allow their lives to be ruined by heroin, would find something else just as effective.

All I know is that as I write this I hope Storm is warm and happy and still as resourceful as ever. I hope he is being loved and taken care of. I hope he is not in the back lanes and fly-pocked rooms of his first three years of life. He, and all like him, deserve so much better.

CHAPTER 7

# CRIMES OF OUR TIMES

IT WAS March 1989 and the registrar at Minda had left a note for me saying that *Sixty Minutes* had called and wanted to do a story. What sort of story, I wondered. It had always been my view that the media should be encouraged to report what was happening in the Children's Court, but they tended not to cover anything except the major cases, which usually involved a young person who had committed murder or some other major crime. Or someone who had done something sensational. A serial Porsche stealer was always top news. There has always been provision in Section 68 of the *Children (Care and Protection) Act 1987* for a juvenile magistrate to allow the media into court. But the Act is specific about the publication of names of children and the broadcasting of proceedings. Provided the child could not be identified by name or picture, there did not seem to be any law or regulation forbidding the presence of cameras or reporters in the courtroom.

Despite this the convention is, even in adult courts, that cameras are generally banned and the only media implements allowed into court are the reporters' notepads and pens, and perhaps an artist's sketchbook. That is fine for newspapers, but to this day, television and radio reporters generally cannot put to air any actuality of what is happening in a courtroom. They have to furiously scribble notes and rush outside to broadcast their radio or television report. But, dealing exclusively with young people on criminal matters, I knew that a lot of this new generation were now getting their information from the electronic media and that newspapers were seen as something that only adults read. It was the brink of the 'video age' and I was seeing before me every day the products of its influence. And I didn't like it. It's fashionable these days to say that impressionable kids should be protected from the extreme violence of some movies and videos, and even the news, but in 1989 it was nothing more than a suspicion that these things were having the influence we now know they have. Yet, being at the coalface of juvenile justice, it was stunningly clear that kids were often acting out what they saw their heroes doing in movies, on television and on videos. And the heroes were often doing things that involved extreme violence. Cutting, gouging, blasting, blowing, twisting, crashing, burning and crushing. By the early 1990s, violent videos had arrived with a vengeance.

I had a meeting in my chambers with the *Sixty Minutes* producer, who outlined in some detail what their intention was. They just wanted to show their two million-plus audience on Sunday night what went on in the Children's Court, warts and all, and they wanted to give me the opportunity to talk about juvenile crime. But they couldn't do it without being given access to the court itself, and they needed to be allowed to film in it. People had to see what was going on, it wasn't enough to just tell them. They promised that none of the kids would be identified, but with this restriction, the day-to-day dramas of the court would be faithfully represented. It was a unique opportunity, but I knew I would have a job and a half to convince the hierarchy that the window should be opened ever so slightly to allow the public to peep in at the workings of the Children's Court. It would be an important move because, to most people, it was a place where someone else's kids went and was steeped in secrecy. I didn't need convincing, but I told the *Sixty Minutes* producer that he would have to be the one to persuade the Department of Community Services and the Chief Magistrate that not only would it make great viewing, but it would also show how tough it was to deal with each young person fairly and judiciously. I also wanted people to realise that 'locking them up and throwing away the key' was not the answer. I so wanted the program to go to air. The time was right. Specifically, I wanted to highlight the problem of disruptive boys being sent to adult gaols because of their violence, even though they weren't eighteen. And generally I wanted people to see how juvenile violence had continued to increase at an alarming rate. But I knew the downside of letting the film crew in—if there was any legitimate complaint about any aspect of the story, I could be for the high jump. I gave approval for the filming to go ahead, and *Sixty Minutes* managed to convince the authorities that the project should proceed.

The whole exercise focussed my mind on what I thought was becoming a huge, systematic problem in the upbringing of children—the video influence. It began in the 1980s, it is endemic in the 1990s and by the year 2000 may well be just about out of control. In the 1980s boys were all wearing American baseball caps the right way around. They were later to wear them back to front. They all took to wearing baggy clothes which fitted them nowhere. On their feet they all wore expensive sneakers. All this took money. Videos and films were showing 'cool' kids prowling around together, identically dressed, making their presence felt—firstly by loud dialogue, then obscenities, then punching the air with their fists and doing Bruce Lee kick boxing. We all thought this new phenomenon was just a fad, a dress fad, and as soon as they got themselves into close-fitting jeans it would all pass. But of course it didn't.

One film, the name of which I have forgotten because there was nothing remarkable about it, showed a gang of young fellows living under railway bridges or in railway tunnels. They were portrayed as modern-day Robin Hoods, stealing so they could feed themselves and their friends. Here in Australia the kids who were watching this stuff were living at home and didn't need to steal to live. The trouble was that, nevertheless, these black American and Hispanic kids became role models for white middle-class Aussie kids. And to this day I don't really know why. Perhaps it's because kids need to identify with something, and with books being out of fashion, videos had taken their place. The easiest targets for these 'heroes' were old people, often women, who were beaten and bashed and often left with broken arms, legs and hips that never healed properly. How I wish now, in retrospect, that we had had the means to make these thoughtless young hoodlums face their victims and look into their lined faces and see the hurt and fear they inflicted. I also wish I had been more severe on some of them, but I knew if I had locked them up at first instance they would have been out on appeal in moments, as all too often happened. I think a lot of superior court judges who overturned the decisions we made in the children's court thought that there were people and places that could simply and immediately rehabilitate these young thugs without them being detained in an institution. But what about them being forced to show some remorse or being forced to accept some responsibility for their actions?

Here's a case I remember that illustrates the point. Drew came before me charged with assaulting a man in his seventies. He had been with three other boys but refused to reveal their names. He came into court dressed in the outfit of the day—the ill-fitting clothes, expensive sneakers and baseball cap. His mother and father were with him. They were respectable, well-dressed, middle-class people. When the case was called, and before anyone could say anything, the mother jumped to her feet and said, 'I'm sorry he's dressed like this, Your Worship. I have his good clothes here,' and she held up a sports bag that carried the name of a prominent private school, 'but he was brought straight from the police station and I wasn't allowed to give them to him so he could get changed.'

It seemed to me she was more aggrieved about her son not being dressed properly than what he and his mates had done. What they had done, however, was dramatically illustrated in the facts sheet handed up to me.

It was the school holidays and the boys had gone to a city cinema complex in George Street, where they had seen a movie about a New York gang who went around frightening elderly homeless people. Then these hoodlums—I call them that even though they went to private schools and came from comfortable homes—had waited around Central Railway Station until they saw a poor down-and-out alcoholic curled up on the grass under a tree in the park over the road. In turn, they each jumped on him and came back and jumped on him again. A passer-by who witnessed it all but who was too frightened to intervene, ran to get help from the railway staff. But in the meantime another man, braver than the first, came to the rescue. Like all cowards when confronted, the kids ran, but this man managed to apprehend Drew. Probably influenced by the 'cool' behaviour of his celluloid heroes, Drew behaved in front of me as he possibly thought they would behave if they were in his expensive shoes. His face showed the disdain he felt for us all. I hated this case for a number of reasons. I didn't need to ask Drew anything but his mother, to my absolute astonishment, said, 'What do people expect when they sleep under trees in the park? They're only asking for trouble.' The father's only contribution was, 'Does Drew's school have to be advised of all this?' I was so angry. I had had a similar case only a couple of weeks before, in which a school captain and vice-captain had bashed an old man dozing in his lounge chair. And for some reason I felt that it would be preferable for Drew's case to be dealt with by another magistrate. It didn't mean I was copping out, but my emotions were so high I didn't feel I could be dispassionate.

Tragically, these sorts of cases are becoming more frequent. Even though quite often magistrates will not have the time to track violent behaviour all the way back to a diet of video, television or movie violence, I'm willing to bet that this, combined with such things as parental breakups, are a major cause of unexplained violence in our community. And it's something that has never happened in history before.

With the unprecedented availability of the video player in many households in Australia, a pattern of video behaviour has emerged. With both parents often working, kids are left at home with the video as a babysitter. The habit often begins in the Christmas holidays, when schoolchildren have six or eight weeks off, but parents only three or four. A relatively cheap and easy way to keep kids amused for the rest of the time is to keep on shelling out money for them to rent videos. Even with the best intentions of the parents, kids get their hands on loud and violent Van Damme or Schwarzenegger-type movies. I don't think one violent video can cause the violent behaviour we saw in Drew's case, but a diet of them certainly can.

I don't believe every kid has to watch nothing but *The Sound of Music* or *The Wizard of Oz*, but if you look closely at some of the most popular videos, the hero is often an extremely violent man who, in the end, is successful in violently outsmarting an equally violent bad guy. I've seen many cases where an older boy, after watching a few of these sorts of videos, will, without reason, pick on a younger boy, who is often doing nothing more than, say, hanging around the corner shop. That's quite often how it starts. It then progresses rapidly to more serious violence, often in gangs. Even during the late 1980s, when I was sitting at Minda, few women travelled by train at night, and even in the day they would not get on a train wearing any obviously valuable jewellery.

Kids don't want to emulate nerds. They want heroes. And there are a lot of 'heroes' in these types of videos. Many kids want power to compensate for something lost at home. They want to feel power, and if they can't be powerful enough alone they'll grab some mates and do something powerful together. And if that means terrorising a trainload of people or an old woman walking down the street, then the buzz is worth it. Or it is to them.

I told all this to Jennifer Byrne and the *Sixty Minutes* team when they arrived for the first of three days filming at Minda. I could see that they thought I was exaggerating a bit when I told them that I believed violent videos were a far more important factor in juvenile crime than most people had imagined. The filming went very well and caused minimum disruption to the court. Sure there were lights and three cameras and lots of microphones, but often you'd forget they were there. At the beginning of each session, I told the court there was a crew filming proceedings, but they would not do so if any party objected. There were very few people who didn't agree to take part. Time and time again kids were brought in and out of the courtroom, and the *Sixty Minutes* people were genuinely interested in what they saw and heard. They also decided that there was a genuine 'angle' in violent videos, and they took me to lunch to decide how they would tackle the issue as part of the program. The first thing I was asked was if I thought that things like television news should be censored to remove violence. I told them then, and still firmly believe it, that you really can't censor television news to the point where you take the violence out. I don't believe that kids are adversely influenced by the actuality of violence in television news and current affairs.

Indeed, perhaps quite the reverse. No matter how badly assaulted or shot or bombed they are, the Van Dammes of the world will live to fight another day—be it in their next movie. But when you see the actuality of a war or the true horror of a car accident—and you know it's real, that the people are really suffering, then perhaps it might do some good. If violent videos did show a victim on a life-support machine with the family gathered around to turn it off, or a victim's funeral, or a boy who became quadriplegic because of a gang beating, then perhaps the cold reality of the real world would get through. If the videos showed perpetrators going through the whole court system, being refused bail, probably being raped and sentenced to lengthy stretches in gaol, then perhaps the videos would have a message. But the consequences of violence are almost universally ignored in these videos.

We decided that, as a way of illustrating my point, we would do some filming in a video shop. I know the producers had a lot of trouble getting a shop to agree, because by this time my views on the subject had appeared in the *Sydney Morning Herald* and other newspapers, and it was beginning to look like a one-woman campaign. But eventually one at Haberfield agreed, and we decided to meet there at 10 a.m. to film a sequence with Jennifer and I walking down racks of videos, perhaps finding one or two extremely violent ones among them. Remember this was an ordinary, suburban video store and I know the producers really didn't expect to find much more than a couple of really bad ones. But when we got there the shelves were full of them. I remember when we filmed I just kept on pulling these videos off the shelf, one by one, and even Jennifer was horrified by some of the titles and subtitles. 'First he kills them, then he chills them,' was one I remember. If it wasn't so serious, you'd laugh.

So what's the answer to the problem of violent videos? Banning them? Prohibition never works, and I think this would cause a huge market in banned violent videos, given that there's such an appetite for them out there. The V chip, which can be used to exclude offensive material from a television? What puritanical nonsense. Kids would easily find their way around these things and there's no point in having an electronic chip do the work of a parent or guardian. There's no easy solution, but I think banning and bugging are no substitute for sound parental control over what kids do watch at home. You have got to change the culture of what kids want to see, and this can only be done by changing the appetite of kids for these things. And this can only be done by adults influencing kids away from violence. Perhaps it's already gone too far, but I hope not. I think if parents and people with responsibility for children really try to change kids' appetites for this sort of viewing, then it is the only way we might get through this disturbing period in history.

The *Sixty Minutes* story went to air and most of the feedback I got was positive. A few of my colleagues thought I shouldn't have allowed cameras anywhere near the interior of the court, but most people thought it was fascinating to see and hear the workings of the Children's Court. The features of the juveniles who appeared in the story had been adequately blurred, and there wasn't, as far as I could see anyway, a negative reaction to the project. The justice system is inherently conservative and the judiciary will always be suspicious of the media, and sometimes this suspicion is deserved, But there's no point in trying to hide our system of justice away from the electronic eye. We're close to the year 2000 and, like it or not, the electronic media is here to stay.

And while we're talking about crimes of our times, there's another social problem that is as old as the written word, but has taken on new and greater significance in the space age. Graffiti. This was always considered a sort of benign and quaint crime, but with the advent of spray cans and Textas, it has developed a potent addiction in some young people which few of us can understand. I saw a lot of graffiti artists while I was on the Bench, and to this day I can't adequately explain their fascination with it. It became so significant that the police formed squads to cope with it and a detective, who was attached to police headquarters, started his own library of 'tags' so he could identify the perpetrators. A 'tag' is a signature that each graffiti artist leaves. Even though it could lead to his identification and arrest, a good graffiti artist cannot stand the torture of anonymity for what he considers his work of art. Around Minda our local graffiti artists were the UTB or United Tongan Boys, and, just like dogs urinating to preserve their territory, the UTBs would 'tag' the perimeter of their territory and it served as a warning to stay out. Do not encroach, do not enter in numbers. Stay out or else. Most of the Samoan and Tongan boys who appeared before me were giants. Their very size was enough to frighten and consequently they did not have much trouble in controlling their home ground. When they ventured out into a shopping centre, everyone was on red alert. The shopping centres countered this by employing security guards, including at least one Pacific Islander.

I had a personal experience with graffiti that I won't forget either. My bank was the National Bank at Campsie and it sported a large, cream, ten-metre wall which was a great temptation for graffiti artists. There'd often be some sort of illustration on the wall, but one day I noticed that the word 'fuque' started appearing there. I smiled because, unusually, this wasn't tagged. A couple of weeks later a young boy was brought into Lidcombe Court, where I sat one day a week. I did not hear any defended criminal matters at Lidcombe, but I could deal with pleas of guilty.

One of the cases I saw was typical of a 'home boy'. All of thirteen or fourteen years old, wearing a synthetic tracksuit, baseball cap on backwards, defiant and not looking in the slightest bit interested.

'The young person,' said the police prosecutor, 'has been charged with malicious damage of the National Bank at Campsie. He defaced the wall running beside the bank with an obscene word, namely "fuck".'

My mind immediately went back to that word 'fuque' I had seen.

I said to the solicitor appearing for the boy, 'Look, just as a matter of interest—and you know I will not be hearing this matter—would you have your client write the offending word on a piece of paper?'

'I can see no reason why not, ma'am,' he said, and gave the young man his pad and pen for this to be done. The result was handed up to me.

'I see,' I said. I turned to the duty solicitor who was representing the boy.

'How does your client intend to plead?' I asked.

'I am instructed that he is not guilty,' he said.

I said to the solicitor, 'As you are aware, I sit at Campsie Court and what you don't know is that I bank at the National. I would recommend to you that you take a look at the unusual spelling we have here and see if you can obtain fresh instructions as to your client's plea. He might just want to change it.'

Later that morning the duty solicitor came back into court with the boy and a change of plea to 'guilty'. It was his first offence and he had finally acknowledged his guilt—with a little help from the Bench.

Generally, however, I found nothing amusing at all about graffiti artists. Millions of dollars are spent every year by governments, state, local and federal, repairing damage caused by graffiti. Owners of some properties have given up repainting their walls because, within twenty-four hours they are ruined again. There were two so-called 'minor' crimes I came to dislike thoroughly during my time on the Bench. One was stripping a stolen motor car—I always felt it was like kicking someone while they were on the ground. The other was graffiti. I believe that graffiti is deliberate, wanton behaviour and that parents should pay for any damage done by their children. And if they can't pay, then they should stand beside their child while the graffiti is scrubbed off. Unfortunately, though, the courts don't have the power to order this.

When I once did suggest that parents should pay for their children's desire to pursue their illegal artform, there was quite a hullabaloo in the media. Critics from welfare organisations lined up to get on air, basically saying that these kids were usually from single-parent families, and how inhumane it would be for the mother to have to pay for it out of her single-parent pension. That is, of course, rubbish. I have seen just as many sons of professional people before me for these offences as I have children of underprivileged families. No matter what their status, parents have probably contributed to the problem by turning a blind eye to some very obvious signs. Kids who have a lot of spray cans and Texta Colours for no obvious reason are, of course, suspect. But many times I found that the parents had been aware of these objects around the house, but had done nothing about it.

How many times did I hear parents say in court in front of their child, 'Everyone is doing it, it is a sign of the times.' My reply always was, 'Well, not everyone is before me, only your son, so there's the rub.' The parents would sometimes say, 'He hopes to break into advertising as a commercial artist.' I had a reply for that as well: 'Well, maybe he should go to an advertising agency and graffiti their walls and show them just how good an artist he is.' So often the parents just did not want to take responsibility for their child's actions.

When a child came before me charged with graffiti-related malicious damage for the first time, my first question always brought a wink from my court staff because they had heard it so many times before.

'Describe the graffiti in your lounge room to me,' I would ask.

Generally, the new young offender would be astonished by the question and not answer. So I'd repeat the question and the response would usually be, 'There's none.'

So I would say, 'And the hall, what's the graffiti like in the hall?'

Again, the child would say, 'There's none.'

'Oh,' I would say, 'and why is this?'

'Because my mother wouldn't let me,' was always the reply.

Putting on my most severe look I'd roar, 'And neither will the public allow you to spray your tag wherever you feel you want to spray it. Do you understand what I'm saying?'

Sometimes it would work. The child had never associated a wall or a fence in public as actually being owned by someone. Having said that, I never gave a graffiti first offender a conviction. I generally let them off under the first offender's provisions and hoped that I wouldn't see them again. I was right in about eighty per cent of the cases. The hard-core graffiti artist was another matter and there were serious, sometimes fatal, consequences of this obsession.

One child who was very dear to my heart became a victim of this peculiar psychological addiction. I knew him personally, through his family. But his big problem was that he didn't seem to be able to stop leaving his tag across Sydney. One Saturday the police rang me at home to tell me he had been critically injured when he tried to crawl through a window of a train to leave his tag on the outside. It seems that you get extra points if your tag is on the outside of a train. The more danger, the more reverence from your fellow artists. Only days beforehand I had spoken to him about the terrible danger of stanchions beside the track suddenly appearing. But this day he boarded a train to the city with a few friends. He had been preparing to climb outside through the window but had only got his head out when the inevitable happened. His head cracked like an egg as the stanchion rammed into it, and he was thrown back into the carriage, blood gushing from his wounds. Instead of trying to stem the flow, his so-called mates left him, not knowing whether he was alive or dead. At the next station they rushed from the train and a guard, alerted by their agitation, found him. He was in a coma and is now brain damaged, paralysed down his right side and has epileptic fits. His life is ruined. He doesn't have the will to continue with the therapy he requires to assist him in everyday living. He was always a kind, gentle kid with lovely eyes. Now those eyes are dulled. He is dull witted and he shuffles along like a lost soul in his oversized, ill-fitting clothes. I often grieve for him and the terrible event that brought him to this at the age of fourteen.

CHAPTER 8

# PERSONAL PLUSES AND MINUSES

WITH MANY jobs you can't just go home and switch off, and my chosen vocation, both as a solicitor and magistrate, was certainly one where you had to live it, or the consequences of it, twenty-four hours a day. As a solicitor, I had always agonised at the end of the day over what had occurred. Could I have done better? Did I put in enough effort? Had I let my client down? These types of questions were not unique to me or to my profession and, I guess, are asked in some way by just about everyone in any job.

I knew that if I continued in this fashion after going to the Bench, I would not last long. So when I was appointed as a magistrate, I made myself a promise—once the key was in the ignition, that was that; I could not change what I had done. At the end of the day, it was time to go home to the warmth of my home and my children. I had to try and leave my work at the courtroom door.

Fortunately in the Children's Court, there is often no time to linger over a child's petty crime. In my early years the cases before me were mostly crime, the care cases would come later. The care cases were the ones that really got to me, probably because they often involved young, utterly helpless babies. In crime, I used to give each child my undivided attention. But I was not going to lose sleep over some kid who had stolen a pair of jeans or had sworn at a police officer—cases which, but for the grace of fate, could possibly have involved any of us.

But there were times when you just couldn't help getting involved. Personally, I have had, as someone else once said, a very fortunate life. I have my natural daughter, Louise, who, at the age of nine, supported me as a 'mature age' law student and my adopted son Jacob, who taught me much about Aboriginal culture, as did Mary, an Aboriginal girl I fostered who has since left home. But also along the way I have had eight, unofficial 'foster' children whom I took into my house for varying periods when I realised there was no way for the system to help them. Each one of the eight is a story in themselves, and to write about them in detail would require another book, so I'd like to use the first child I took home, Cindy, as an illustration.

When I was a solicitor in the 1970s, children who habitually wagged school very often ended up in a detention centre. The philosophy of those days was very much, 'If you don't go to school then we'll educate you at a detention centre', and I really hated the idea of kids who wagged school being forced to mix with juvenile criminals. Cindy lived on a new estate at Campbelltown with her mum and dad. The problem was that her parents had been the victims of a complex real estate agreement with a local developer, where they were paying an exorbitant weekly rental for a pretty inferior house. They had been conned, legally, but didn't know any better. They were conscientious and trying to work their way out of this debt, but they were so busy that Cindy got very little of their attention.

Cindy was a cheeky, bright, fair-headed kid who got up at 5.45 a.m. with mum and dad, dressed for school and waved her parents goodbye as they headed off for work. Then, sitting in her school uniform, she would watch TV all day. She wasn't really alone in this, as most kids on the estate were in the same boat. Their parents just weren't around and the rate of truancy was staggering. Unfortunately, the parents simply couldn't give their children the supervision they needed. There was very little local work and most of the parents had to drive fifty-two kilometres to Sydney down a double-lane 'highway'. One breakdown and they were lucky to make it home before midnight. The welfare of the kids on this estate was in the hands of a lone Department of Community Services district officer, who was so underresourced that he had no choice but to bring the waggers to court and recommend they go to the Reiby Detention Centre. I was the duty solicitor at Albion Street Children's Court, and when Cindy ended up there I represented her. The magistrate had let her return home twice before, but on the third occasion I knew that he would send her away—a nice, innocent, but totally unmotivated fourteen-year-old. In the foyer of the court, I spoke to the officer before the case started.

'I think you know what the magistrate is going to do,' I said to him, 'but don't you think it's disgraceful that Cindy should be locked up for, literally, doing nothing? There must be a better way.'

He shook his head and said, somewhat dismissively, 'Yes ... so do you know what the answer is?' I knew the officer was frustrated by Cindy, by me and by the system, and he wanted me to stop asking questions he couldn't answer. Questions to which there were no apparent solutions. There were just a few moments before we were due in court for me to come up with this magical answer. Cindy's mother, bearing all the signs of overwork and lacking sleep, was sitting next to her, frantic at the thought of her daughter going to an institution. I turned to her.

'Look,' I said, 'you know this is Cindy's third time and I'm pretty sure the magistrate will send her away unless we do something radical.

'I'm sure he really doesn't want to do that, but he's afraid of what might happen to her alone in your house on the estate every day. We've also got to make sure she gets an education.' Then came the crunch. I didn't really know what I was doing, but instinctively, emotionally, it felt right.

'So this is what I suggest. How about she comes to me from Sunday night to Friday night? You can pick her up for the weekends on your way home. It is the only way I can think of for us to save her from an institution.'

The mother was desperate. Like any mother, she didn't like the fact that she couldn't take care of her child, but giving up work was not an alternative. Even with just the court cases she'd taken too much time off work, and she couldn't afford to have her wages docked.

She looked at me, with a sort of hopelessness that attacked my heart. 'We've got nothing to lose,' she said.

We presented our proposal to the magistrate, who seemed relieved that he had not been forced to make a decision that could ruin a young life, and Cindy came home to my house. This was after Louise had gone overseas on a working holiday to Asia. So it was just me, Jacob and Cindy.

There were a few hiccups, but Cindy soon got into the routine of getting up at a decent hour, showering, having breakfast and cutting her lunch. I drove her to school for the first two weeks and in no time at all she got into the habit of going to school. I had enrolled Cindy at South Strathfield High School where an old chum from my school days at Fort Street High School, was principal, and under his watchful eye she blossomed and eventually got her School Certificate. Cindy was with me for ten months. But I must say that I never really attached to kids like Cindy and my other short-term, unofficial 'foster' kids, nor they to me. We both knew they went home for weekends and would eventually go home for good. We liked each other and were able to live in the same house, but when it was time for them to move on, and they did, there was no pain and anguish. It was funny, however, that I never wanted to take a child home once I went on to the Bench. I think it had to do with my sitting back and coming up with an answer without getting personally involved. Overall, I look on my experiences with these kids as something really positive in my life, and my helping them personally was something the system would never be able to do.

There were, however, quite a few personal negatives in my professional life as well. I suppose it stems from others deciding to involve you in their life because of what they perceive you have done to them by reason of your position. Juvenile justice is *per se* a huge emotional roller-coaster for those involved in it, and when emotions run at boiling point strange things can happen. At its extreme, this has been shown with the horrific violence displayed towards Family Court judges in New South Wales. These judges are, of course, only doing their jobs, but their jobs are to try to be fair when each person in an emotionally charged case thinks they have right on their side. In the opinion of those parents, to find otherwise—in other words, against them—is unjust and unfair. But, unfortunately, someone has to lose, and when that someone is emotionally unstable, it can lead to calamity.

And while the Children's Court did not have anything as bad as the violence shown to the Family Court, we did have our share of problems. I had one in particular—a man called Clancy. He ended up almost making me lose my mind.

I first saw Clancy when he, his wife, and three daughters appeared before me at Minda.

This family had lived in a big town in southern New South Wales, and a year previously the local magistrate had taken the girls away from their parents because it was alleged they had been dabbling in the occult and had been heavily involved in Devil worship. They also lived an itinerant lifestyle, their various homes ranging from a sleazy private hotel to a pricey Paddington terrace, all depending on Dad's income at the time.

The magistrate had obviously believed that the allegations were so serious he made the children wards of the state, and ordered Clancy and his wife to undergo psychiatric counselling. The couple moved to Sydney and now, after a year, I had to decide whether the children should go back to their parents. But as I saw it, nothing had changed. The parents were still dabbling in the occult, still itinerant and Clancy still did not have permanent employment. The five of them sat behind their lawyer—a young man in the regulation black pinstriped suit who occasionally glanced around at Clancy. Clancy was a very tall and striking man, who oozed confidence. He was wearing a business suit, but his shirt was slightly crumpled, his tie wasn't in the best taste and, overall, his appearance somehow missed something. Even before the case had formally begun he was constantly tapping his solicitor on the shoulder and making notes. His family was quite a contrast. His wife was extremely thin with hollow cheeks and was wearing a very plain cotton dress and sandals. Her hair was mousy and long. She looked anorexic. The oldest girl was six. Like their mother, the children were all very pale. They sat quietly looking sad and forlorn. I wondered if they were terrified of their bombastic father.

Even as his solicitor rose to his feet to announce his appearance, Clancy interrupted. As usual in these cases, the children were represented by the duty solicitor, but Clancy shouted out, 'My solicitor represents my whole family.'

'Please be seated, Mr Clancy,' I told him sternly, wanting to lay down the ground rules from the start. 'Your solicitor will speak for you. In this court, children are represented separately from their parents, and that does not necessarily mean that there is conflict between your solicitor and the solicitor for your children. It is just that the children's interests are better served by independent and separate representation.'

Clancy sat down. His solicitor tried again.

'Your Worship,' he said, 'on the instructions of my client I would apply that the wardship order not be extended, but rather that the order on the three children be rescinded and the care and control of the children returned to the parents. If Your Worship does not think both parents should have the children, then I would ask that the father be given custody.'

The solicitor then began to detail why the children should be allowed back. He said they had a home to go to and his client had taken out a two-year lease on that address at a rent his client could afford. Arrangements had been made for the children to attend the local school and nursery. Their mother had been advised there was part-time work for her in one of those 'alternative' shops that sell incense and the like, so she could be at home for her children after school.

But Clancy really was one of those clients who constantly interrupted his solicitor. Whenever the solicitor rose to his feet, Clancy was continually passing him notes. It appeared as though he thought that not only was he in full control of his case, but of the court itself. He was very intimidating and a person whom I disliked instantly. I've no doubt that he perceived that I didn't like him, and whether that had anything to do with what happened later, I have no idea. He was a man with nothing to recommend him. He spoke instead of his solicitor, he spoke for his solicitor, and when I wouldn't answer him or when I wouldn't recognise him, he would then ask his lawyer for permission to speak. He delayed the proceedings at every opportunity.

When he was called to give evidence to support his application, it unfolded that the man was an unmitigated liar. He was unable to produce any lease documents, there was no letter to support his claim that his wife had the promise of a job, nor was there any confirmation of a job for himself. There was no letter from any school in the area, or nursery, concerning the children. But even under stringent cross-examination by the solicitor for the department, and the childrens' solicitor, Clancy refused to back down.

Then it emerged that he and his wife were still very much involved in the occult. He claimed to have some powers, but he said that it was his wife who was the witch in the family—a most unlikely looking witch—and that two of their daughters had shown definite signs of following in their mother's footsteps. His wife never gave evidence so it was difficult to uncover any more details, not that I thought I needed many. Try as hard as I could to keep an open mind about this, I found it very difficult.

And then, for me, the horror began. Clancy started stalking me. I have never been quite so frightened in my life. This occurred in 1988, when there were no stalking laws and it was very difficult to find anything illegal about someone just watching you. After his case had been adjourned for the second time, Clancy began to appear regularly in the hallway outside my chambers. He did not intimidate me in any way by approaching, he just stood there—smiling. By the third or fourth occasion I had begun to feel definitely uncomfortable. I mentioned it to a clerk at Minda, who hadn't been involved in the case. She brought it to the attention of the court constable who, that day, asked Clancy to leave, which he did. Then a few days later as I walked down the passage to the tearoom, behind a fence which separated the staff from the children and their parents, there he was waiting for me again. As I walked near the fence he came and leant against it, again just staring at me.

Some evenings when I worked back I would go to get into my car when there weren't many people around and he would be standing there just looking at me. It got so bad that I used to worry about him following me home because I did not want him to find out where I lived. I started changing the way I went home, all the while watching my rear-vision mirror. It was becoming an obsession, whether he was there or not.

We had fire alarms at Minda, which could be triggered by large red buttons in the corridors. Late one afternoon, when there were only four or five of us left in the building, for the first time that I can remember all the alarms went off, and the fire brigade and police arrived very quickly. But there was no fire. I walked to the front door of the court complex and looked out and there across the road was Clancy, just standing there smiling. We had no doubt he was the one who had pressed the button and caused the alarm.

The next day I confided in a policeman who wasn't connected to the court and said I thought I had become obsessed about this. He thought it was right for me to be deeply concerned. He said it was not beyond imagination that Clancy had set off the alarms to time how long it took the police to get to court late in the afternoon, when there weren't many people around, with the possibility of doing me some harm.

Then a couple of weeks later, one Saturday I was driving to do my shopping when I glanced in the rear-vision mirror, and there he was driving the car behind me. I started to shake. He was doing nothing I could complain about legally, but he was having the time of his weird life. Eventually he drew level with me and turned his head, and looking at me smiled his usual macabre smile. I was too frightened to be angry.

On the Monday after work, I went straight to Burwood police station. I was a mess and trembling, half-crying, half-laughing collapsed into a chair. I said, 'You're going to think I'm an idiot but …' and the whole story poured out. The detective I saw was most understanding and explained, and I knew he was right, that there wasn't a thing anyone could do. He gave me his private phone number so I knew where I could reach him at all times, and he promised to put on two extra patrols in my street. Somehow it filled me with confidence and I went home feeling much better. Of course I had not passed my fear on to the children because I didn't want them to be frightened.

That night, I kissed Jacob and Mary goodnight and went to bed. Then I heard it—a quiet tick, tick, tick. Oh God, I thought, he's got into the house and somehow planted a bomb. I woke up the kids. We searched the room and Jacob went outside and came back laughing—Mary had turned on the washing machine and the sound was that of the water meter. But that was the state to which Clancy had reduced me. I thought I couldn't go on with this case because I couldn't be impartial. I decided I would ring the Chief Magistrate, Rod Blackmore, and explain the situation to him. But fate intervened and in the end I need not have worried. I discovered that Clancy had complained, via his solicitor, that he had overheard the solicitor for the children and me discussing the case outside the court which, of course, was a legal no-no. It wasn't true, but it was a perfect opportunity for me. I had no hesitation in disqualifying myself and handed the matter over to another juvenile magistrate.

Clancy complained to the New South Wales Law Society, he complained to the New South Wales Attorney-General, he complained to the Premier and anyone else he could think of. But the matter had been transferred to another court and I was no longer hounded. This man terrified everybody. I later heard of a district officer who became involved with the case and who eventually had a nervous breakdown over it. She had to be sent on leave. The magistrate who eventually heard the case, unbelievably to me, granted an order giving Clancy custody of the three girls.

Fate intervened yet again, however, and the month after he had been given the children, he got quite a large amount of money as a result of a lottery win. With his winnings he took off and went to Scotland, leaving his wife and the three little girls here. I've never heard of him again. The mother decided to devote herself to being a good witch and came back to court to surrender the girls. She had never really wanted the responsibility of them and now she was rid of her husband she wanted total freedom. But as things turned out the girls were in luck. They were able to return to the foster parents who had looked after them during the time they had been made wards and who loved them dearly. They settled back into family life very quickly.

When I was appointed to the Bench I knew there would be constraints on my life, and I made another promise to myself. I would never be seen anywhere my presence could be misinterpreted, and that meant, like other magistrates and judges, I had to be very careful about which functions I attended. I was supercautious. I didn't want my photo taken at, let's say, a football match where, unbeknown to me, a well-known criminal was sitting in the row in front of me. I had a small, close circle of friends with whom I associated. Dinners, the opera, the movies and suchlike were always with them. I also had to be very careful with security, as Clancy had taught me early in the piece. I was wary about giving out my home address and, of course, my number never appeared in the telephone book. I thought it would be very difficult for anyone with whom I had to deal to get my address—but one incident showed me that you can never guarantee such a thing.

Pumpkin was the name of our family cat who, like every cat I ever had, was a stray. He was a big dope of a ginger cat who loved cuddles and would often crawl on to your lap for a snuggle and a purr. The horror of what happened one Sunday morning in 1988 still haunts me. I opened up our front door and just about tripped over Pumpkin, who was normally never there. He was lying on the door mat stretched out on his side, not attempting to move. I knelt down to pat him and said, 'What's up Pumpkin?' and to my horror I saw what was wrong. Pumpkin's left paw had had a metal butcher's hook shoved through it. Then the hook had been pushed under his chin and into his mouth and had emerged through his cheek. Blood trickled down his fur and over the mat. This horrific act had been performed on our doorstep or on the front lawn, and then poor old Pumpkin had been dumped where we couldn't miss him. I froze when I saw him. If he had been a human being I would, of course, have called an ambulance, but I didn't know what to do with that old and faithful little cat. I didn't want to move him with the risk of the hook causing further injury. I rushed back inside and called the police. By this time both Jacob and Mary had come out to investigate and the three of us, distraught about this horrible, wanton cruelty, could do nothing but wait. Within ten minutes a police car had arrived, with a sergeant and a young officer, who seemed almost as upset as me.

'I'm calling the rescue squad,' the sergeant said. They arrived in amazingly fast time in a big white rescue truck and they brought in a large net and long protective gloves, but Pumpkin was too hurt to cause them any concern. He had gone into shock and was paralysed on the doorstep. One of the rescue squad constables had gone to the van by this time and came back with a pair of bolt cutters and quickly snapped through the hook. He pulled it out and we made arrangements to get Pumpkin to the local vet.

'Do you have any enemies?' the Sergeant asked.

'I'm a Children's Court magistrate,' I said, still in a bit of shock myself. But I didn't have to explain more.

'I see, well, that's it then,' said the Sergeant, opening up his notebook. Once again patrols in my street were stepped up to twice a night and once again I felt the personal vulnerability of my job. Pumpkin did survive but he was never the same, happy-go-lucky fellow he once was.

I guess such things are a hazard of the profession. And while they were rare, and fear was not an emotion that ever dominated my thoughts or decisions, the sad fact is that you did have to be aware of the potential danger that could arise in just about any situation.

It could happen anywhere, any time. Jacob needed new cricket boots and we set off one Saturday morning along Burwood Road, a busy high street teeming with people and, you'd think, pretty safe. Jacob, however, suddenly had a sixth sense about something.

'I think, Mum, that two boys are following us,' he said. I half-turned and glanced and, yes, he was right.

'Yeah,' I said, 'I feel them … I think I can see who they are.'

The sports shop was on the other side of the road, but just as we were about to step off the gutter to go there, there was a tap on my shoulder.

He was about fifteen, neither big nor small in size, wearing 'grunge' gear with the compulsory Reeboks on his feet, but missing the usual baseball cap on his crew cut.

He was straightforward. 'Hey, Judge,' he said, 'Can I ask you something? Why did you lock me up?'

I recognised him from a case I had dealt with a couple of months before; the circumstances are irrelevant here.

I thought it through in a millisecond and decided the best approach was absolute candour. I felt no fear of this little punk. I told him without showing any emotion:

'You know why I locked you up. You got a month more than your mate because you had been in trouble before and I warned you then.'

He stepped closer, so close I could smell his steamy breath that contained an odour of pot or alcohol or both. His mate, however, was somewhat less enthusiastic about a high street confrontation. He grabbed his friend's shoulder and cautioned, 'Just cool it, man. Let her go. It's not the time.'

But the kid continued, 'No way, it wasn't fair.'

By now his body was peripherally jerking and quivering, and from the corner of my eye I could see his hands spasmodically opening and closing, like a boxer just before a bout.

I was wearing a large topaz ring and I thought, 'If this kid hits me I am going to hit him back.' It was, of course, quite silly. If this kid had hit me, one punch and I would have been out for the count. His friend was screaming, and I waited for what appeared to be the inevitable blow. The weird thing to me, as I remember, was that people were passing by, they could see the danger to me, but they just kept on going. Salvation came in the form of a siren. For some reason a police car came screaming down Burwood Road. Its effect was immediate. Like a bolt of lightning, this sound seemed to electrify both these boys. They looked in the direction of the police car and took off down the street as fast as they could. I wasn't, I don't think visibly upset. Nor was Jacob. He seemed to believe that magistrates, in particular his mum, had power over everything. They would suffer no harm. Then it dawned on him that there might just have been a need for a fight. He thought about it for a minute.

'Okay,' he said, 'if you want to go a couple of rounds in Burwood Road, we'd better go to Newtown Police Boys Club and let Jeff Fenech give you a few lessons.'

Jake got his cricket boots. I forget what they were. But they were whatever brand he asked for.

CHAPTER 9

# THE DRAMA OF A DROMEDARY

THEY SAY that a camel is a horse designed by a committee, and if that is the case then there should have been a hump instead of the Coat of Arms outside Burwood Local Court. It was 1991, and finally someone in the Attorney-General's Department decided that Minda had had its day, and even with the Band-aid improvements we had made to the tawdry old building, it just wouldn't do. The Attorney-General's Department was building a new complex of six courts in Belmore Street, Burwood. As the building progressed they realised that they only needed four adult courts and so decided they would kill two children's courts with one stone and move both Minda and another children's court, Royalstone (which had taken over from Yasmar) from Glebe to Burwood. From the beginning, however, the complex was never designed with children in mind. That meant that those of us with collectively thousands of hours of experience in running children's courts were not asked to comment on whether this new place was at all appropriate for its new purpose, or how it could be changed for the better. We knew it really wasn't going to work, and we (meaning myself and many of the solicitors involved with the Children's Court system) decided to let the then Attorney-General, John Dowd, know of our concerns. There was a lot of letter writing, and on 22 April that year I received a reply from Mr Dowd which I hoped would put our fears to rest. When I opened the letter, however, it was clear that he didn't understand our concerns.

> *Whilst it cannot be denied that children and adults will inevitably encounter each other in various parts of the building, this is no more than what occurs to a far greater degree each day in many courts throughout the state. However, the children's courts will occupy a distinct part of the building, special accommodation will be available to FACS (Family and Community Services) to look after young children involved in care cases and there will be a special, separate counter area for Children's Court matters.*
>
> *I believe the small compromises necessary to locate the Children's Court in the Burwood complex are justified by the opportunity to provide a more accessible and convenient location, more comfortable facilities for all users of the building and the gain the advantages of having two children's magistrates sitting together brings.*
>
> *Thank you for taking the trouble to write to me on this matter.*

Mr Dowd might have thought his 'compromises' were 'small', but we all knew they were mammoth. Burwood was all steel, carpets and windows and bristling with security, but the nightmare started each morning just trying to get into the place. There was a secure, grey concrete car park beneath the complex, and the magistrates had all been given security beepers with which to open the door. It was a far cry from parking at the rear of Minda and climbing up the stairs to the back entrance of the court. At Burwood, every morning without fail I would be terrified that the door would come down on my car when I was only halfway through. Instinctively, I would duck each time I drove in or out. It was really quite stupid that I began my day of bowing at learned counsel with bowing at a bloody car park door. I used to feel so silly—but finally, one day the door did come down on the bonnet of one of my fellow magistrate's brand-new government cars. His Worship was not amused, but nothing was changed. Once we were inside and the door came down, we were sealed tight in the car park, with even more doors and locks with secret security timers to get into the courts.

The adult prisoners were brought across from cells in Burwood police station next door and were taken along a corridor to court. The trouble was that to get to our chambers we had to cross this corridor, and it was not considered a good idea for magistrates and prisoners to meet. So a peculiar system was designed involving two doors, a metre and a half apart, which would block off the corridor and allow the magistrates access to their chambers. Each door had a handle and in addition there was a timing device. The trick was to open the second door before the first one had closed in order to beat the timing device. Once the first door had closed and you couldn't open the second one in time, you were locked in. It made me a nervous wreck every morning and I'd taken to propping the first door open with a brick which I kept hidden in the car park, which then had to be moved once the second door opened. I then kept the second door open with my handbag while I put the brick back into the car park, ready for its work that afternoon when the whole performance was reversed.

Finally it happened though. A poor magistrate and a court registrar had been stuck one morning, unable to get help and suffering terrible claustrophobia. There was no alarm in there and the only way they would have been found was if somebody had opened the door. There was no-one to hear their shouts from down in the basement, so between them they had been forced to kick down the door back into the car park. Our regular chant became, 'We hate this bloody place.' Every day without fail one of us would say it.

In keeping with the disaster it became, it was fitting that Burwood did not get off to an auspicious start. On opening day, I was standing next to one of the tea tables with a friend of mine, Pat O'Shane, who was another woman magistrate. We were waiting for the Attorney-General to arrive when one of his minders rushed up breathlessly and said, 'The Attorney's running ten minutes late. Could you ladies not serve the tea until he gets here?'

Pat and I just stood there with our mouths open, and it dawned on both of us at about the same time what was happening. Even though this man was from the office of the Attorney-General, he could not envisage how two women by themselves next to a tea table could be anything but tea ladies, let alone magistrates. It hit him at about the same time as well, and we noticed him turning red.

'Oh my God,' he said looking at Pat, 'you're a magistrate.' Then he looked at me. 'And so are you,' he sort of whimpered.

He was incapable of saying anything else and just took off into the crowd. It made our day, how we laughed and laughed, but we didn't see the poor guy again all day.

While there was all that security at the back of the building, the front was a different matter for the public. For some inexplicable reason they had put the Children's Court on the first floor, and here was the second nightmare. We had more than one near tragedy when children due to appear in court climbed onto the first floor balcony and threatened to throw themselves off into the lane. In the case of the younger children, there was the threat of them leaning out too far over the balcony and falling.

The first floor was open plan with adult courts on two sides and the Children's Court on a third side. The fourth side opened up over downstairs like a sort of a mezzanine level. The result was that while children were to be protected by remaining anonymous when appearing in court and required special treatment, at Burwood not only did they mingle with adults, but there was no separate witness room. So we had sexually abused teenagers sitting in the same area as those people they had accused of abusing them. It was a complete disaster.

The other Children's Court magistrate there was John 'Joc' Crawford, who was equally concerned about how inappropriate the whole place was for juveniles. Joc was a tower of strength in those days. We both realised that we had to get used to all this because there was a job to do, but it didn't make life any easier. There were thirty-two uncarpeted concrete steps from my chambers to the courtroom and another plastic card that opened the door into court—a door that opened outwards directly onto the stairs. When approaching the door you had to hope there was no-one about to exit the court or you would end up taking a nasty tumble. My leg never healed properly after I broke it while at Minda, and by the time I got up those concrete steps, and onto the Bench every morning it would be giving me so much pain.

But as much as the venue had changed, unfortunately they were still the same sad cases and the same faces at the Bar Table. One of my first cases at Burwood concerned a part-Aboriginal boy, Lionel, who had appeared before me six months earlier at Minda.

I really hadn't expected to see him again. His mother, an articulate, intelligent Aboriginal woman with a high-profile government job, had also been with him on that occasion. Lionel had then been charged with what is commonly called shoplifting, but is legally called stealing, from a retail store. His mother had said they didn't need to be represented by a solicitor from the Aboriginal Legal Service and she would speak for him, which she had done very competently. She stood in front of me and she spoke clearly and firmly:

'He's never been in trouble before. He was with some other boys and it was a bit of a dare really. The T-shirt was the wrong size for him and he certainly doesn't need T-shirts anyway.

'That boy is going to learn a lesson from this. He won't do it again.' She appeared determined and I believed her.

Lionel was a lad who had attended high school regularly. He was a fine sportsman and I could see no reason to give him a criminal record. So I had dealt with the matter under Section 33(1)(a) of the *Children (Criminal Proceedings) Act 1987.* I found the offence proved, but in all the circumstances I dismissed it. This was a section of the relevant Act that I used quite often for first offenders.

But here Lionel was in front of me again, this time charged with assault, malicious damage and resisting arrest. They were very serious charges and I must say, they surprised me. Lionel had denied the charges and this time his mother had instructed counsel to appear for him.

The children's courts in Burwood were identical to the adults' courts, except the magistrate's benches had been lowered so that we appeared less lofty and intimidating to the children. But the whole atmosphere was still antiseptic. The place was painted grey. Boring blue-grey. There was a long Bar Table for counsel, and a separate table for witnesses. What was peculiar and very annoying for just about everyone was that the chairs were bolted to the floor, even those at the Bar Table, so everyone was stuck in place, as though they were glued to the floor.

The police prosecutor, Brian, who had come with us from Minda, called the first witness, a woman employed by the State Rail Authority as a station attendant. When she was called she came marching like a soldier through the grey double doors and strutted her way to the witness table. She wasn't wearing an SRA uniform but she might as well have been. She wore a white blouse and black skirt for her day in court and it was easy to see that she was not an easy-going person. Indeed, if you were to use one word to describe her, it would have to be 'officious'. I gave her the benefit of the doubt, however, putting her manner down to nerves. She took the oath on the Bible and began to give her evidence.

She had been on duty on a Friday night at 11.45 p.m. at a western suburb railway station. As you'd expect for a Friday night at that time, the platform was awash with teenagers, both boys and girls, who had been to the local raceway and were waiting for their trains home. They had been well behaved and nothing untoward occurred until Lionel walked towards a rubbish bin.

Without expression, the witness continued in a staccato fashion that suggested to me that she had been practising:

'This young person approached the rubbish bin. He had a chips bag in his hand which he put to his mouth, blew it up and then burst it. I approached the young person and said. "Did you make that noise?" He laughed and said, "Yes."

'I said, "Come with me." He said, "What for?"

'I said, "That's for me to know and you to find out."

'The young person said, "I'm not coming." I then took hold of the young person by the arm and he roughly pulled his arm away.

'I grabbed his arm again and called to the other station attendant for assistance.

'He then took hold of the young person's other arm and together we attempted to take him to the station master's office. The young person resisted violently. At the time he was uttering the words complained of.'

Brian said, 'Are you able to repeat those words?'

She said, 'Yes. The words were, "Fuck off". We proceeded on either side of the young person, and as we attempted to enter the station master's office he grabbed the door and refused to enter. Finally the other attendant was able to free his hand from the door and attempted to place him in a chair. But he was struggling so violently that the chair fell backwards and he hit his head.

'The young person then got up, raised his fists and told my colleague to have a go.'

The story continued. By this time a lot of young people had congregated outside the station master's office door and, of course, in all the excitement had been egging Lionel on and calling these two railway employees by every name they could lay their tongues to. It was a riot.

Then the local constabulary had arrived, taken Lionel with them and the 'audience' had got on the various trains and gone home.

At the police station Lionel had been charged with offensive behaviour, offensive language, two counts of assault and malicious damage because the door apparently was damaged. And on it went.

Once Brian had finished taking the station attendant through her story, what is legally called her evidence-in-chief, there were some points I wanted to clear up right away. I turned to the barrister who was appearing for Lionel and who was ready to cross-examine her.

'Just so that I can understand exactly the position on the railway station, do you mind if I ask a couple of questions, so I've got it in my mind what the picture was before you ask your questions?' I asked him.

'Certainly, ma'am,' he said.

I turned my attention to the woman and cleared my throat.

'Now you correct me if I'm wrong, Lionel walked to a rubbish bin?' I asked her.

'Yes.'

'You saw him do that?'

'Yes'

'He blew up an empty chips bag and popped it?'

'Yes.'

'What did he do with the chips bag?'

'He put it in the garbage bin.'

'Can you please tell me what was the offensive behaviour at that stage that you are complaining of?' I asked.

'It was a loud bang,' she said.

The prosecution case went downhill from then on. It was apparent that this whole situation had got out of hand, not because of a wrongdoing on Lionel's part, but because he had dared to challenge a woman who wanted to exercise unnecessary authority over someone she saw as vulnerable. I felt he probably received the treatment he did from this woman because he was Aboriginal. But that wasn't the only reason that I was angry. The situation got worse when Lionel was taken to the police station. It turned out he had no money. All he had was his return train ticket. By the time he was released from the police station, the trains had ceased to run and he had to walk five kilometres home. This clearly was a case where just about everyone in authority was negligent in their duty of care to a child. If the police had been thorough in their investigations, they would have told the woman that there was no law against blowing up a paper bag and that the whole thing had come about because of her attitude.

It was quite a lecture that I delivered, not only to this woman, but also to the police. I spent so much time on that Bench attempting to bridge the gap between the police and young people, that when I saw what I believed to be injustices or thoughtlessness like this, I became dispirited.

I did come across some police who worked tirelessly and took some pretty awful verbal abuse from kids which they overlooked in their effort to bridge the gap. Then you would get one, and it only took one, to undo all the good that nine or ten others had done. I dismissed all the charges, the assaults, the offensive behaviour, the malicious damage, but I correctly guessed that Lionel's mother wouldn't leave it there. She later took her own action in relation to what occurred that night and heads rolled, as they deserved to.

Lionel might have thought that justice had been done, but one thing he didn't know was something I think is very unfair. Although the charges were dismissed, under the system they were placed on his record card with the word 'dismissed' beside them. This meant that if he appeared in court again, it would be known that he had made a previous court appearance, and a magistrate could wonder why the charges had been dismissed—even though he was required to ignore them.

Another thing Lionel didn't know was that I was somewhat of an expert, in a personal sense, in prejudice.

Every Friday night I would eat out with Jacob and Mary, and we took it in turns choosing where we ate. One of our favourite spots was just around the corner. The restaurant was owned by people who had been friends of mine for over twenty years and they treated the children like family. This particular Friday it was just after Christmas. These friends always gave the children a loaf of stale bread to feed the ducks in Burwood Park, so this night, as usual, they took themselves off to the park after dinner with their stale bread. Usually it was at least half an hour before we saw them again. But this particular night they were back within ten minutes. Jacob was wide eyed and puzzled.

'We really didn't do anything wrong, we really didn't,' he burst out. 'We were just feeding the ducks and Mary was getting this duck to follow her.'

Every Christmas a lot of these ducks were stolen and ended up as Christmas dinners. It was really sad and pathetic, especially since ducks mate for life, and so after Christmas some of them would be wandering up the street looking for their lost mate.

When Jacob and Mary had calmed down, I found out what had happened. Mary got the duck to follow her, using the bread as bait, but two policemen happened to be passing in a paddy wagon. They parked and walked over to the children.

'Do you kids live around here?' they asked.

Jacob said they lived not far away and the officers, looking at each other with what I am sure was a superior look on their faces, asked 'Do you like duck, do you?'

Mary said, 'Yes, we do like ducks.'

One of the policemen, trying to trick the kids, said, 'Yes, I heard Mum had a duck for Christmas dinner.'

Mary said, 'No we didn't, we went to a hotel with Mummy and Louise for Christmas and they didn't have duck.'

He said, 'Where was the hotel? Redfern?'

Mary said, 'No, no, it was the Intercontinental in Sydney.'

He said, 'Well, I have to get your names and addresses, because we've had a lot of complaints about you children stealing ducks to take home to your mum. I suppose you sit round the campfire, do you?'

Jacob and Mary were nine years old. In their innocence they said, 'We have a stove.'

Jacob said, 'And our mum would never steal anything because she's a magistrate and she'd get into terrible trouble.'

Telling his story to me in all his innocence, Jacob said, 'And Mum, they must have been going to check up on us because they ran and got in their wagon, and didn't come back.'

It wasn't until years later when they were well into their teens that the significance of that story dawned on the pair of them. I'd brought them up to be totally trusting of police and explained that, 'They are always your friends.'

It was through similar experiences that Jacob more than Mary found there were some police who weren't his friends and never would be due to their prejudices.

Other police, however, were marvellous, like the Sergeant with a sense of humour who had to cope with three excited kids who thought they had found a treasure trove. This was the day that Jacob and Mary and their friend Pete were playing cricket at the local school when Mary went off looking in some giant oil drums that were used as recycling bins. She found a couple of jewellery boxes, called out to Jacob and Pete, and the three of them went through the bins, finding watches, brooches and earrings. It was fairly cheap jewellery, but a treasure trove to kids their age.

They came bolting home to me with it, as excited as can be. I said it was probably a robbery from some jewellery store and the thieves had most likely discarded this stuff because it had no real value. They agreed with me that we should go to the police and hand in the jewellery, because there was probably some shopowner who was out of pocket. I had nothing to do with it because it was their find and I felt it would do them good to handle it themselves. All I did was drive them to Burwood police station, sat on the station's waiting-room bench and left them to it.

They walked up to the counter, Jacob and Mary with black skin, black curly hair and black eyes, and Pete with very fair skin, red hair and freckles. They were quite a colourful threesome. To greet them was this wonderful Sergeant, a big man with a ruddy face, lovely smile and very friendly to kids.

'Well Sir, what can we do for you?' he said to Jacob.

Jacob blurted out, 'We found these and we found them in the garbage bins at the school and we think they're from a robbery.'

He said, 'Right, you might be right. Sir, you'd better give me your name.'

'Jacob Holborow.'

'And your address?' Which Jacob dutifully told.

Then the officer asked Mary her name and address.

'Mary Holborow,' she said, 'I live at the same address.'

Then he looked at Pete and said, 'I'll take two guesses. One is, you're not a Holborow.'

Jacob said, 'How can you tell?'

I burst into laughter and had to leave the police station as the sergeant, grinning at the kids said, 'I deal with a lot of people mate, and it was just a hunch.'

Because of my Aboriginal children, no-one thought me prejudiced. I always tried to treat everyone who entered my courtroom with dignity. Sometimes, however, it was a bit difficult, and one of those times involved a woman who had come before me at Burwood because the authorities thought she couldn't cope with her large brood of kids. They had been alerted to her through the school because her eldest child turned up looking dirty and unkempt. The mother was ordered to appear before me so I could make an assessment, but I didn't have to look up from my reports to know that she had arrived. There were simultaneous sniffings and whispers of things like, 'Oh, God' from the Bar Table and it took just a few milliseconds more for every non-essential person to head for the door. The reason for their sudden exodus became clear when the odour of the mother, her five-year-old daughter and her toddler wafted to the Bench. At Burwood there was a little gate from the Bench to the monitor's desk that allowed me access to the courtroom. Every second child used to swing on that gate, so I decided to leave it open because I didn't like children to be restricted in the court. This toddler thought it great fun to run up to my chair and then jump down the steps through the gate, but she was wearing a disposable nappy that had needed changing for at least two hours.

After reading the evidence, I decided a quick solution was required. I had no intention of taking the children away from their mother. It was clear she just needed some professional help—and a little education in hygiene. I told her, rather breathlessly, that I would finish with the case that day so there would be no need for them to come back. The mother was relieved and so grateful that she stood right in front of the Bench and picked up her toddler. Holding her out to me she said, 'Say goodbye to the kind lady.'

The little girl put out both her arms as if for me to take

her. I would never refuse a child, but in this case I couldn't bring myself to take the little girl.

'She wants to give you a kiss,' said the mother.

'Oh, no, it's all right, she doesn't have to kiss me,' I said.

But the mother walked around the Bench and up the steps and pushed her toddler up to my shoulder.

'Kiss the kind lady goodbye,' she said.

I gave the child a kiss, but I nearly suffocated. Everyone who was left in the courtroom knew what the matter was, but they withheld their laughter out of courtesy for the mother. After that I always kept a spray bottle of perfume on the Bench, just in case.

That morning we needed to take morning tea early, just to let some air into the court. The only alternative to the hated cement stairs was for me to walk out into the public carpeted area and take the lift to the ground floor where chambers were. It was a bit of a security problem so my monitor would accompany me, either making sure we were the only two in the lift or scrutinising those who were with us. It was more than just a security problem for me—it represented yet one more thing wrong with the complex itself. One time in the lift, I pressed the button and turned around to see a little girl smiling up at me who had just been before me because it was alleged her mother was neglecting her. I looked around, and just before the lift doors closed I spotted the mother out on the veranda smoking, totally unaware her child had wandered off. I took the girl back up in the lift, handed her to an official and gave the mother a few facts of life.

That episode really disturbed me, because I thought if we had an irate father, or indeed anyone who wanted custody of a child and had been denied it, or indeed, if there was a pervert in the building, they could just get in the lift and take a child with them without anyone noticing. The public area was like a Turkish bazaar most days, with adults and juveniles packed in shoulder to shoulder.

Burwood was not a happy place for any of the Children's Court staff, as I have said. We had been used to having our own court and at Burwood we felt like little fish thrown into Manly Aquarium. I'd only ever sat alone, but here I was one of six magistrates. They were friendly, but we tried to keep the courts separate. Children should not have been mixing with adults, as they did in this complex. It certainly was not a relaxed place to work.

I had managed to persuade the powers that be to give us a nursery and one office was vacated to make room. The nursery was well equipped thanks to the Department of Community Services, but it was too small and on a different floor from the court.

For me, the last straw that, in this case, broke the camel's back was another incident involving the lift. I'd pressed the button and as the doors were closing, a little fella of three who had just been sitting on my knee in court recognised me and ran after me. I couldn't find the button to keep the doors open quickly enough and I was terrified the doors would close on him because he may have been too slight to keep them open. His mother was screaming and everyone turned to look. All I could see was a potential tragedy. I dashed forward and scooped him up as the doors closed behind us. That was it for me. We had all been complaining and writing letters to the relevant authorities about how unsuitable the place was. It wasn't only me who complained, so also did the duty solicitors, the Department of Community Services officers and the police and sheriff's officers. They all had concerns. Even children's welfare groups had taken up the cry. But despite this loud and powerful protest, there wasn't even a hint that something was going to be done. There was only one course and that was to make the situation as public as we could.

I walked straight from handing the child to his mother to picking up the phone. I threw all caution to the wind and at the same time put my career on the line. I rang up radio station 2UE—I can't even remember who I spoke to—and told them I was a magistrate and wanted to go on air. Such requests were unheard of and the producers were quick to give me a hearing. My frustrations came pouring out. And I didn't stop at one radio station. As soon as I had hung up from one, I rang another. In the afternoon, there were television news interviews. Burwood was rather like the Olympic Games media centre and I was about to be awarded a gold medal, in the form of a new court, or alternatively a termination notice. The next morning I was summoned to see the Chief Magistrate, who made it clear over the phone that he didn't approve of all the kerfuffle. I didn't go to see him. Some of my fellow magistrates also weren't too happy about my public outbursts and decided that the correct course for them was to pretend I didn't exist. Magistrates have never been encouraged to speak out, even though they deal with social issues every day. The knowledge they had gained was to be quarantined inside the courtroom and not allowed into the outside world where it would have some value. I'd been asking for years for a special court to deal with care cases, but it took my public outbursts to get action.

Of course, I wasn't the only one doing the complaining. Soon after that others went public as well. One of the solicitors revealed to a local newspaper what was going on in the bowels of the building, where the cells were. Although the adults and juveniles were in separate cells, the cells were next to each other, and the juveniles were subjected to crude, uncouth comments and mockery and threats from the adults. The solicitor was quoted as saying:

> *Children are being traumatised by having to appear in the same court as hardened adult offenders. The children are scared, anxious and threatened. On one occasion children had to be escorted over vomit left by an adult drug offender. Children are complaining of being uncertain and frightened*

*by the large number of gun-carrying police. Police don't wear guns in children's courts, but they do here and it intimidates and frightens the children. The noise and cramped, cattle-yard like conditions at Burwood Court have a very unsettling effect on the children.*

The outcry was so loud that something just had to happen. Soon after, I received a phone call from the Minister for Justice, Terry Griffith.

'G'day,' he said.

'G'day yourself,' I said, expecting a blast. But instead he asked me what he could do to make me 'happy'.

'Give me a specialist care court,' I said, 'and I promise we won't complain again.'

I waited to see what would happen.

CHAPTER 10

# THOSE TRACKS ON MY FACE

I REMEMBER the pride I felt when I first walked from Campsie Street through the brick portico and into the foyer of the revamped Campsie Court. This court had been the old Petty Sessions Court covering Campsie and surrounding suburbs since early this century. But such were the renovations, that to me there was not a ghost of an old lag in the place. I still felt though that the new green wooden sign over the front gate, which said Campsie Children's Court, didn't say enough. To me, it should have been Campsie Care Court, with Care being the ingredient that made it really special—and made a certain amount of public agitation (agitation which to some was nothing more than 'more mischief by the Holborow woman') worthwhile. Here, finally, was a court that specialised in the care of kids who were victims. A court whose primary role was not to deal with the perpetrators of crime or neglect, but to help those who had become the victims of them. I hoped desperately that the pervading attitude of this court would not be one of punishment, but of understanding and sympathy. My experience of Minda and then of Burwood had really left a bad taste in my mouth and I was hoping Campsie would be a toothbrush with heaps of toothpaste on top. Of course there were a lot of people who were responsible for its existence, but I couldn't help thinking that my very public outbursts had helped do the trick.

It was extraordinary how fast things moved after my telephone call from Terry Griffith telling me that everything had been okayed for a care court. Suddenly $500,000 had been allocated just about overnight. The timing of my 'mischief', together with the overwhelming support for change by the juvenile duty solicitors who attended the court day in and day out, had been auspicious. A climate of public criticism had been created—specifically around the disaster of the Children's Court at Burwood, and generally about how the Government was not doing enough to help neglected children. The political will of change was there. So if ever the then-Liberal state Government wanted to score some points, it was with Campsie Children's Court. Unlike Burwood, the authorities had even consulted with magistrates, registrars and court clerks. Submissions were called for, architects on overtime drew and redrew, builders and painters suddenly arrived and then, there it was. There was nothing Dickensian about Campsie. The building was bright and sunny and welcoming. There was a large waiting area, freshly painted and carpeted with bold furnishings. Walls had been knocked down to make some areas larger and built to make other rooms smaller, according to the need. Even our morning tea room was beautifully furnished and equipped.

The courtroom wasn't large but it had high ceilings which gave it an airy feel. It was like no other courtroom in Australia. The design was taken so seriously that I was visited by a colour consultant and the result was a courtroom that had an atmosphere of calm. The main colours were heritage Federation pink and blue with a Laura Ashley floral print up the first metre of every wall. The Bench was only two small steps off the ground so I didn't sit up high in judgment. There was no witness box. Instead we had a modern table and chair with a microphone so people didn't feel intimidated. The atmosphere was good; it was friendly, warm and non-threatening.

I sat four days a week while Joc Crawford, my colleague and friend, sat at Campsie on Thursdays. Joc had moved from Burwood to Lidcombe Children's Court, which heard the criminal matters, and then each Thursday we swapped.

I had wanted a good atmosphere at Campsie and it certainly seemed to have worked. Kids used to skip into court and were relaxed dealing with me.

The court got off to what I'll call an interesting start. It was Friday, 4 December 1992, a sunny day for the grand opening which was staged by the Government so the court would get the maximum publicity. By this stage Terry Griffith had become Minister for Police and the court was officially opened by Wayne Merton, the Minister for Justice and Emergency Services. Out the front there were tea and scones and lots of local dignitaries and members of the local media. A grand political opening in the grand old-fashioned style.

We were packed like sardines into the courtroom for the opening ceremony; every seat was full and every standing spot was taken. I was very excited and elated.

Then the Honourable Minister began his speech, and as I listened it became apparent that he was talking about Campsie as though it were a criminal court and not a care court. And while he might not have appreciated the difference between a children's care court and a children's criminal court, it was the very essence of what we had all been working for. To me, professionally, it was my *raison d'être.* I was sitting at the side of the courtroom next to the head children's court magistrate, Rod Blackmore. I was so furious that I just wanted to storm out and I half got to my feet. Rod grabbed my arm and stopped what could have been a great newspaper headline and some sort of political incident.

To me, the glamour of the day was tarnished. It disappointed not only me, but every member of the staff at

Campsie Children's Court. It appeared that once again the politicians had missed the point. Most of the staff from Minda had remained with us and moved across to Campsie, while staff from other courts had specifically requested to be part of the new care court. As they all sat proudly in the audience on this, our big day, I could feel their puzzlement and then anger that the Minister didn't mention, that not only was this care court unique in Sydney, it was unique in Australia and possibly the world.

But politics and speeches aside, once we got down to business I realised we had something very special here. It was an entire court that focussed on the many needs of children, where proper representations could be made on behalf of both the children and their families in surroundings which were anything but imposing.

Within a week the court was functioning well. All the care cases that would have been funnelled into Burwood Court came to Campsie and this meant that every child from the moment of birth until the age of eighteen (in reality sixteen), and who was notified as a child at risk, would be referred to Campsie Court. The 'catchment area' for these cases began at Palm Beach to the north of Sydney, extended west to Liverpool and south almost to Sutherland. It was quite a tall order. But the thing that really stood out in this court was that you never saw a police officer. Generally, if the police were called to an incident of, say, domestic violence, and children were considered at risk, the police would contact the Department of Community Services (DOCS). The police would either wait at the scene or take the children to a police station and deliver them to the DOCS officer. (I use the expression 'deliver' on purpose, because the expression 'hand over', from a juvenile justice point of view, has criminal connotations.) Overnight, the DOCS officer would take them to what was known as 'a place of safety'—an emergency foster parent used in short-term crises. The law required that the children be brought before a court within seventy-two hours, if it hadn't been decided that the problem was relatively minor and the children could be returned home safely. If the matter was serious, then what would generally happen was that the DOCS officer would arrange the appearance in court, by first lodging a complaint stating the ground or grounds that caused the children or child to be brought before the court. No matter how old the child was, a duty solicitor would be appointed to look after their interests. This was the preferred procedure in all cases in New South Wales, but it was from here on that Campsie, we hoped, would really make a difference—not only for the child but for the family as a whole.

One of the first and most unusual cases I had to deal with at Campsie was Ellie. I wonder what she felt as she looked across at me. She was twenty-three and a lovely looking Aboriginal woman. She had fine features and a gamine Audrey Hepburn look. I remember her in a dress of white cheesecloth and she looked very striking. She also had three children under school age and a serious kidney condition that meant her going into hospital to have one kidney removed, or possibly both, with the necessity of a kidney transplant. Then she would probably have to spend a year convalescing. The problem was what to do with her children while she was recovering.

Ellie was sitting on a chair behind her duty solicitor and directly behind her on the front row of seats was another woman who was her mother, Maureen. Unlike Ellie, Maureen was making a fashion statement, and on a score of one to ten she scored ten and a half. She was wearing a floral dress of red and black and her hat was a sight to behold. It was big and black and sweeping across the wide brim and then falling down to her shoulder was a large crimson feather from a long-deceased beast of unknown origin. She looked magnificent. Both mother and daughter were from a little town just outside a large city in northern New South Wales, and they had travelled by train for their day in court to obtain what they hoped would be justice. The DOCS solicitor referred to a document that had been faxed to him from the local office:

'Your Worship, Ellie had planned to leave her children with their maternal grandmother and the last time she had come down to Sydney for tests for her upcoming operation, she had contacted the Department of Community Services for advice. They had spoken to certain authorities in Ellie's home town, which is a small place and Ellie's mother was known to them. After inquiries, my department has come to the view that it cannot approve the maternal grandmother being the sole carer of the children and accordingly cannot approve the application.

'The primary problem appears to be that the maternal grandmother had herself had children from a young age and was not involved in their upbringing because they were removed from her care.

'The maternal grandmother has, however, maintained contact with Ellie, and it appears that a trust has developed between them.

'Now obviously Ellie herself, given the nature of the surgery, will not be able to take care of her children. If Your Worship feels that the grandmother cannot take care of them adequately, then they will have to be put in foster care.

'It is up to Your Worship to decide.'

Well, I thought to myself, it might be a new and wonderful court, but they certainly weren't new and wonderful problems.

It had been my experience that a lot of Aboriginal women, even in these days, had allowed their children to be taken away by authorities who did not understand their culture. Maybe not forcibly, but too easily. Often they weren't sure of their rights, and some didn't care to find out about them, so they didn't put up a fight. In Maureen's day, she wouldn't have even had anywhere to go for advice—except of course, to the people who took her children away. It meant that on paper, these grandmothers looked as though they hadn't been too good as mothers because their children had been removed from their care. But they loved their children, and if the help had been there for them, in my books the children would not have been removed. So whenever I was told that an Aboriginal grandmother had been a bad mother to her own children, I wanted to know more. I wanted to know how and I wanted to know whether this was information that had been handed down from one district officer to another district officer who was new to the area and had never known these women. But now, when these mothers became grandmothers, not only had they learned personally from their own terrible experience, but they had learned they had rights and they could stand up and be heard. They had learned they could prevent their daughters and their sons having to go through what they went through if they stood up and were counted. This is exactly what this grandmother, Maureen, wanted to do and she had challenged the district officers to show exactly what she had done wrong. She stood there eye to eye with them in the courtroom for them to prove that she was not a fit grandmother.

I needed to hear from Ellie herself and she was called to the witness 'table' where she took the oath and got comfortable in the seat. I wanted to know about the father of her children, who happened to be white, and why he couldn't look after the children while she was in hospital as other fathers would do. So she started to tell me about her life with him, and as she spoke she fixed her eyes on a point on the wall just above me, as if she were embarrassed and pretending in the middle of this courtroom that there was no-one listening. She spoke as if she were speaking to herself, or into a tape-recorder.

It became apparent as she spoke quietly that he was a brute who, while he didn't touch his children, came home drunk most nights and beat her.

'He comes home and he belts me bad,' she said in a tiny, almost embarrassed voice.

'I have to go to the doctor sometimes. He gives me pills and things and he helps me with my cuts, but it always happens again. It always does.'

'Ellie, why don't you leave him?' I asked her when she finished speaking.

This time she looked directly at me. 'Too far to town,' she said.

I didn't need to ask any more. That said it all. 'Too far to town.' It meant it was all too hard for her, and once she had got into the small country town, where did she go then? She had been with him since the age of fifteen and he had beaten her so often, she just accepted it and could see no way of escape.

Maureen did not look much older than my own daughter and, as a mother, I thought it said a lot about her that she had accompanied her daughter and supported her through all this.

I let the children go and stay with their grandmother. I feel that a lot of district officers dealing with Aboriginal people, particularly those stationed in big cities, have no concept of the way of life of these people, to whom time means little and the extended family means everything. Their love of the outdoors can affect the tidiness of the inside, a standard so often important to district officers.

I was impressed with the grandmother and felt it was important for the children to stay with their family wherever possible. As I was to discover later, I turned out to be right.

While I was sitting in my new chambers deciding what to do about Ellie, I thought back to an Aboriginal girl I had known when I was a solicitor. The memories brought back a mixture of emotions for me. It was in the days when I was the duty solicitor at Sydney's original children's court, Albion Street, working on the duty roster. It was kind of fun to not know exactly what the day would bring and who you might be representing, and I remembered I was somewhat taken aback when Kylie was brought into the interview room. She was only twelve, and a little undernourished Aboriginal girl who had been living in stables at Canterbury, where a number of trotters were kept. The Department of Community Services had brought Kylie before the court on a complaint of her being exposed to moral danger. I found it hard to keep the smile off my face when I heard the details emerge in court. I challenged the department to prove that the horses were immoral and therefore posed a danger to my client's morals. I remember the magistrate was amused, God he was a nice bloke, but the department was not—and nor was I when I saw what had been happening to this child.

Kylie and I took an instant attachment to each other. I phoned her mother, who was from the north coast, and explained Kylie's position. Her mother was employed on a property as a cook and was a hard-working woman whom, I am sure had had a hard life. She and I talked for some time and she said that it would be okay with 'the missus', meaning her boss, if Kylie came home, but she didn't think she would stay because there wasn't much for her to do. With great naivety, I organised for Kylie to return to her mother and considered the case closed and that everyone would live happily ever after. I am much wiser now and I guess that today, I could have predicted what would have happened.

Within months Kylie was back at court. This time she had been found sleeping in a park and this time the magistrate found she was indeed exposed to moral danger. This case occurred quite early in my career, and until Kylie I had never been to Bidura Girls Shelter, which was at Glebe where Bidura Courthouse now stands. Although I really didn't need to have further legal instructions from Kylie, I had a need to see her.

Armed with some goodies, but no cigarettes, I went to Bidura and asked if I could have a legal visit with my client. I was not made to feel very welcome, but I persevered and was exposed to a lecture from the matron as to most of her experiences with Aboriginal girls, and how they should have a special place for them because they corrupted the other girls. I found it hard to imagine little Kylie corrupting anybody; she was so small, so defenceless and so guileless.

Anyway, she was summoned and came to the matron's office, where I was waiting. We were both told we could have time together in a room down the hall. As I left the waiting area with Kylie she whispered, 'Miss Barbara, could you take your shoes off please?'

I whispered back, 'Yes, but why Kylie?'

And she said, 'Because your shoes will make a mark and it's my job to keep this hall clean.'

The hall was spotless. Not a speck of dirt to be seen. This little thirteen-year-old Aboriginal girl whose only crime was that she wanted to sleep in the open, had polished that hall on her hands and knees. Maybe I could have understood it if it had been 1874 but it was 1974 and as far as I could see we had not come one jot closer to understanding children, especially Aboriginal children.

So she and I sat like mother and daughter, talking. Just talking. I had handed over the goodies to matron, but I told Kylie that I wanted her to get them from matron and that if she wasn't given them, I would be asking matron why when I next visited her.

Now that I have been a magistrate, I realise how difficult it must have been for the magistrate hearing her case. We all knew Kylie was not a criminal. She had never committed a criminal offence. Her only 'crime' was that she wouldn't stay in any one place. I wonder now, looking back, what would have happened if I had taken her home with me. Would she have stayed with me? I don't know. I like to think she would have but I don't know. Much to my sorrow, the magistrate committed her to Minda for six months. I tried to come to terms with it by saying at least she'd be getting a bed to sleep in and would be safe. But when I visited her at Minda shelter, I was appalled. I was appalled at the coldness of the place, the lack of love, the lack of physical contact.

As I sat with Kylie on an area of grass which was used by the girls when they were visited by their parents or relations, I was struck by something strange about a row of doors. There was just something not right about them. Then I realised—there were no door handles. These rooms were used for the girls who played up, and were where they would stay until they had quietened down. As well as no door handles, there also weren't any eye-level windows—they were all up at the top of the rooms. I know the jobs of the matron and the staff were not easy and they couldn't show affection to one girl without showing affection to them all, but maybe they should have shown affection to them all. Maybe it's easy to say now, but I can't imagine any girl coming out of Minda at that time who wouldn't be scarred for the rest of her life by her stay there.

Kylie used to tell everybody that I was her mother, that I had adopted her a long time ago and that when she was released, she was coming home to live with me. She even had a photograph of me with Jacob when he was a baby and she would say he was her brother. Then one day when I was at Minda Court appearing for another child, a message came across from the girls' shelter asking if I could go across because Kylie was in a terrible state. I remember I ran. When I got there, this little girl was hysterical. She was screaming, she was beating her fists and sobbing uncontrollably. When she saw me she came and threw herself at me. When I had quietened her I said, 'Tell me what has happened to you, tell me.'

She replied, 'Queenie's dead.'

I knew Queenie was her fifteen-year-old sister and I asked her how it had happened. She said Queenie had had a baby that morning and she had died but the baby lived. I thought of her mother who was the cook on the station and how she would be reacting to this tragic news. Would she claim her grandchild as her own, or let the welfare look after that baby as she was letting the welfare look after both of her own daughters?

Kylie became convinced that she had to get this baby and care for it because it was her responsibility. I was able to calm her down and I promised that I would make all the investigations that I could, but that I didn't think it was possible for her to raise this child. I made many phone calls, but the child had already been taken into care and to this day I don't know what became of the baby. I do know that the grandmother never came forward to attempt to claim her.

Kylie eventually left Minda and went out of my life for about six months. She came back when she was about fifteen. This time it was really serious. She had been drunk and then she had been raped. It was the inevitability of it all that made me so sad. That and the hopelessness of it, because I couldn't see a light at the end of the tunnel at all. Kylie was committed to an institution for another six months and then said that she wanted to go home to her mother. I had this feeling, strange as it may sound, that she knew she was going to die and she wanted to go home to be with her mother. It was absurd, I told myself, there was nothing wrong with the child. Yet Kylie had a terrible sadness about her. I said I would do whatever I could to help her go home, and I organised through Department of Community Services for a train pass for her to go to the north coast when she finished her time in the institution.

She never made it home to her mother. Something happened on the train that caused her to be arrested and she was taken and placed in a police cell. She had been dead a month by the time I was told. She had died of lead poisoning. I was told that the lead was contained in the paint flakes in the police cell where she had been held for some considerable time, because there had been no-one to bail her out, no children's court in the close vicinity and no escorts available to take her further afield. How she had ingested the paint and over what period of time this had occurred, I never knew.

Thankfully this wouldn't happen now because children are no longer held in adult cells, and they have to appear before a court very soon after their apprehension. To that end, things have improved vastly for the Kylies of this world. But that is cold comfort to me when I remember that little Aboriginal girl who told everyone I was her mum and whom I did truly love.

As a solicitor, I saw many young girls who had either left or run away from home in the country and come to the bright lights of Sydney. Some bright lights! But they tended to be good girls and it was the boredom of country life and the lack of work that attracted them to Sydney. When they got to Sydney, however, there was nowhere appropriate for them to live. I had this idea. I had noticed a building in Annandale that had previously housed English migrants and their families and was now standing empty. It had two storeys and to my view lent itself admirably to a girls' hostel. I suppose I had something in mind like a mini-YWCA and I envisaged the girls would be able to go to school, if they had interrupted their schooling to come to Sydney, or go to work and remain there until they could find some other accommodation. I was very definite in my idea that a married couple should live on the premises twenty-four hours a day to be there to support and direct the girls.

It was then I encountered Rex Jackson, the Minister for Community Services, who often used to see himself as the most glittering of rough diamonds. He had been a ward of the state himself and knew what it was like. He kept saying he wanted to do what he could to help underprivileged kids get on. Rex himself had achieved much by just becoming a Minister of the Crown. But later, of course, he went from fame to infamy when he was gaoled for corruption after he changed ministries and became responsible for prisons.

But the day I arranged an appointment with him to discuss my plan to provide safe accommodation for girls from the country, his fall from grace was future history. He was still working in lavish style with elegant accommodation in Macquarie Street and greeted me with affection when I was ushered in to his office. We shared a cup of tea out of lovely china cups and he listened with compassion, I thought at the time. I had written a number of letters to his department and he had been well briefed. He explained that as the building had been used for migrants, it was a federally owned property and so there was nothing he could do about it. He thanked me for my interest and was very pleasant. Yet as I left Parliament House, it was with very mixed feelings. I felt I was yet again a victim of expedient politics. This was a political answer, and it appeared to me he couldn't care less about a problem which, twenty-five years ago, was forcing young girls from a country background on to the streets of a cosmopolitan and dangerous city. How could anyone who was a minister responsible for children let it lie there? Didn't he know what the situation was with these young girls?

When I got back to my office I began telephoning Canberra, and I continued to telephone Canberra over the next few months until eventually I was advised that the federal Government really didn't want this building and would be only too pleased to rid themselves of it and lease it to the New South Wales Government. How naive I was! Excitedly, I made yet another appointment with Rex Jackson and, just as pleasant as ever, he offered me a cup of tea and explained very patiently that I didn't know how these things worked. Money was allotted and allocated for projects years in advance, and of course this had not been included into the next year's finances, and so accordingly the welfare department, as always, was too strapped for money to take up the federal offer. He concluded by saying that anyway, he had to care for lots of children, not just girls who had run away from their homes in the country.

I had declined his offer of tea when I saw the way the conversation was going, and as I walked out of his rooms and down the corridor, I reflected on his nickname 'Buckets', not knowing then that he had earned the moniker because he delighted in dropping 'buckets' on members of the opposition in Parliament. Anyway, I gave it my own meaning—he was a bucketful of hot air and I would have tipped a bucketful of something else over him if I had been given the chance.

Rex Jackson had turned being pleasant and offering cups of tea into an art form.

My disillusionment with the political system was so complete that I was never to ask anything of another politician until 1992, when my dream of a care court came true. Terry Griffith was a compassionate Minister and really did seem to care, and I'm sure it was because of his enthusiasm that Campsie came into being. But it was slowly becoming apparent that in the world of child abuse and neglect things weren't getting much better. Within six months of my two years on the Bench at Campsie, I had heard cases that broke my heart. An eight-year-old girl assaulted by her father and left with severe bruises on both her legs; a fifteen-year-old slapped and punched in the face by her father; a baby aged just eight months who was transferred from the country to Sydney by air ambulance, in a critical but stable condition suffering from haemorrhaging to his retina and other head injuries consistent with the 'shaking baby' syndrome.

There was the two-year-old girl airlifted from the country with a fractured skull and other fractures to various parts of her body as well as much bruising. I had been told she would be left with some brain damage and a weakness down the left side of her body. Her mother and her de facto husband were charged with assault.

An eight-year-old girl told me that her stepfather had slapped her face and struck her on the buttocks with a large metal spoon. He cut off her hair for speaking to her mother's counsellor and physically abused her up to three times a week.

One eighteen-month-old child had been admitted to hospital after being found unconscious in the backyard of his home. He had bruises, both new and old, to his face, arms and legs and torso. He also had a right subdural haematoma, excessive fluid to the brain and retinal haemorrhages. He had signs of internal bleeding.

Another eighteen-month-old child was airlifted, again from the country to Sydney, with a perforated bowel and other intestinal injuries caused by sustained beatings. Doctors had to operate to remove his appendix, part of the large and small intestines and part of the colon. It led to renal failure and he was placed on a dialysis machine. Bone scans revealed various old fractures.

I saw a seven-year-old girl with welt marks across her back who said her father, although really it was her uncle, had hit her with an electrical cord in a beating that had been so severe, it drew blood.

The mother of a nine-year-old girl had left her daughter in the care of a man whom the child knew only by his Christian name. Once the mother had left, this man chased her through the house, tearing off her clothing. She locked herself in the bathroom but he kicked the door down. He removed the rest of her clothes, tied her to a bed and sexually penetrated her four times.

One thirteen-year-old I saw revealed her mother had abused her and her ten-year-old sister. It turned out the mother's de facto had beaten and kicked them and that the thirteen-year-old had been previously sexually assaulted by a male relative. An older sister confirmed the story.

A fourteen-year-old girl was kicked to the ground by her father who then wrapped a telephone cord around her neck and attempted to strangle her. I could see her neck and left thigh were badly bruised and X-rays revealed a fractured bone in her neck. Her three-year-old brother had a fractured arm and his sister, aged two, had extensive bruising varying in colour and size across her face and ears.

The father of another brother and sister, aged fourteen and twelve, was charged with assault after they told how he hit them with a machete. A fourteen-year-old refused to return home after stating she was belted and verbally abused by her parents, particularly by her mother who used whatever was at hand, including kitchen utensils, to strike her. An eleven-year-old girl and her three siblings came before me after her mother had committed suicide when it was revealed the eleven-year-old was being sexually abused by her father.

There was the case of a twelve-year-old who refused to go home because she was forced to sleep on a mattress in the laundry without blankets, and on two occasions had slept on the floor of the garden shed. She had bruises across her body where her mother and stepfather had beaten her with a length of garden hose. Her father was dead and her mother had been refused residency in Australia. The case ended when the mother went back to Italy taking the child with her, despite the fact the child was at the time in the care of the Department of Community Services.

A seven-year-old girl told me that a man, known to her only as John, had touched her breasts and vagina on several occasions while her mother was present. She said her mother had given her alcohol and Valium and had twice stuck her with a hypodermic needle.

Another abused child, aged four, came before me after his doctor had seen extensive bruising on his right ear, both thighs and buttocks. His lower lip and forehead were swollen and he was malnourished. He had told the district officer that his mother's de facto hit him with a belt and often made him stand in the corner for long periods of time, including overnight. Another father used an electric cattle prodder to discipline his two sons, aged seven and ten.

There were the four sisters, aged seven years, five years, one year and three months, who walked into a police station one day. The elder two were carrying the younger girls and told police they had run away because they were scared of their father. He threw them around the room and made them stand in the corner for extended periods. The older two had carried their baby sisters with them because they were afraid their father would hit them. They told police their mother could not help them and they had seen their father assault their mother. When interviewed, the mother confirmed the children's story.

There was a fourteen-year-old girl who had been assaulted by her mother's nineteen-year-old de facto. He had dragged her from the backyard into the house, fondled her breasts and tried to remove her clothes. Her mother arrived home in the middle of the attack and blamed her daughter for instigating the incident. She kicked her daughter out and the terrified girl went to a local store and called 000 for help.

Then there were the eleven-month-old twins who were air-lifted to Sydney from the country where they had been staying with relations because their parents were in gaol. The twins had both been beaten and one was found to have a severe injury to the left side of his head, subdural haematomas, swelling to the brain and retinal haematomas.

He weighed only 6.8 kilos and was immediately placed on a life-support machine. I had made him a ward of court so he could have all the treatment that was required without having to seek the permission of the parents each time, which would have been difficult as they were in gaol. One morning his doctor rang me at court to say that he felt that the life-support machine should be turned off, allowing him to die. This was one decision I felt that only the parents had the right to make, so I convened a court at the hospital. In a small room near the intensive care ward, there was the solicitor for the child, both the parents and the paternal grandmother. The little fellow lay in his cot, hooked up to his life-support machine with a maze of tubes. We were not able to see the side of his head where he had been struck because of the way he was lying. He looked a normal, healthy little baby.

I was concerned about the father who was very agitated. He had a violent history, and I was afraid he would say or do something that would get him sent back to gaol before I had released the baby from wardship and the court hearing was over. I told the grandmother that I would like to speak to her son alone with his wife and her words stuck in my mind.

'Now look, dear,' she said. 'He's very dangerous. He can be looking at you and seem fine one moment and attack you the next.'

It was a risk I had to take. Although there were prison guards, I did not want them in the room because I knew I wouldn't be able to speak properly to the couple. It was with some trepidation that I asked the guards to leave, but I need not have worried. The father was like a lamb. He showed no aggression at all. I wanted to explain to them exactly what was happening.

'I've organised for you to be here today because you know your baby is going to die,' I said. It was no easier saying it with both parents in gaol than it would have been had they been living in a suburban home. It was not the time to dwell on the fact that had they been at home looking after their twins, this would most likely never have happened.

'The doctors want to turn the machine off, but I don't want anybody but you to give them that authority because the baby is yours. It is your right as his parents to say yes, turn the machine off. I don't want it coming from the department, I don't want it coming from me, I want it coming from you,' I said.

They were both so calm. With his arm around his wife, the father said, 'Yeah, yeah we should, 'cos he's ours.'

I told them he had still been theirs while he was a ward of court and how I had done that only so he could get proper hospital treatment.

I rescinded the wardship order and made an order the child remain in the care of his parents. We stood around the bed and the parents sat with their hands on their son. Then the doctor turned off the machine and we all stood quietly. In half an hour the baby died.

Those were the type of matters that I had before me daily at Campsie.

Heartbreaking and frightening.

It became apparent to me that, while I was seeing the young victims' side of it all at the care court, when it came to the criminal courts, the victims' side was not really being told. It was obvious in my time at Campsie how often clever lawyers did not allow judges and juries to see and hear what I often saw and heard. Often, the sentences that were dished out to people who had caused youngsters extraordinary pain and suffering were totally inadequate and did nothing to protect the child or children from further abuse.

The reason being, if an adult was the victim of an assault he would quite often be called by the prosecution to give evidence about what happened, and the jury would be able to see for themselves what the effect of a crime has upon someone. With good reason, children were not encouraged to appear in the formality of an adult court, and in any case many were too young to speak. I did my own informal study to compare sentences given for crimes against children to similar crimes against adults. There were far more instances of a '556A'— the most lenient form of sentence, which effectively meant no punishment at all if there was no reoffending within a specified time (and no record as well)—given to offenders against children compared with offenders against adults. They would be able to walk away from their actions without any criminal record. It used to make me sick.

There were, however, moments that gave me great happiness and amusement at Campsie. There was young Jasmine. Jasmine's mother, for a number of reasons, was not able to care for her properly and Jasmine had been placed in foster care. Her mother was also confused about whether she could adequately cope with a girl of four. Jasmine had been in foster care for a month while reports had been completed so the case was back before me for an adjournment. It was necessary, however, during the adjournment, which would be for a few weeks or even months, to either return Jasmine to her foster family or start looking for long-term accommodation.

Jasmine was a beautiful little girl and sat there, solicitor by her side, looking far too wise for her years. She had long, dark hair and looked fit and certainly not in need of a good meal. To look at her, there was no hint that she was, in fact, a very neglected child and had been neglected for quite some time. She had not been physically or sexually abused. She had not been deprived of food or warmth or a comfortable home in which to live. But her story, like a lot of other children of her background, her ethnic background, was not unfamiliar to me. At the age of fifteen her mother had come to Australia to marry a man she had never met. He was a man she only knew to be older than her and who, according to the correspondence received by her father, was able to work and provide for her and to give her many sons. Soon after she arrived in Sydney she was married and not long after that, she was pregnant. But instead of producing a son, she produced Jasmine.

Her husband moved away from their small unit in one of the inner-city suburbs, but maintained his marital right to return whenever he felt so inclined to claim his bed as her husband. Jasmine's mother was still only seventeen and a most attractive young woman. She soon found that she appealed to a number of men, and in her loneliness and isolation she turned to these other men for company.

If it had not been for the ever-watchful eye of a neighbour, Jasmine would never have come to notice. I doubt that pre-school or even school would have picked up what was happening to her. While her mother entertained, Jasmine would be left in another room to play by herself. As her mother did not have a telephone in the unit and it was necessary to make phone calls from a public phone box some distance away, Jasmine was often left in the unit alone while her mum popped out.

When Jasmine had come before the court, the mother had had no opposition to her being removed from her care for a short period while she considered her position and what would be in her own and Jasmine's best interests. It hadn't been difficult to find a short-term placement for such a sweet little girl, but however good the family was, it was not her real mother who was there. Now I had to decide where Jasmine would live. I had become concerned as to whether or not she was fretting for her mother, despite what the district officer's reports told me. After reading the reports and listening to the officer, I told the mother and Jasmine's solicitor that I'd like to have a little chat with Jasmine so we could find out what she wanted. I explained this to Jasmine and with the permission of all concerned, I walked down from the Bench and put out my hand to the little girl. Holding hands, we walked into my chambers where I pulled my chair from behind its desk and sat Jasmine in the chair opposite me.

I explained that I really did have a magic wand and I could grant her wish in relation to where she was going to spend the next short while; maybe with her mother, maybe with her foster parent or maybe in some other lovely home. As I spoke along that vein, Jasmine never took her eyes off my face. I thought to myself, 'This is extraordinary for a four-year-old. I've got this little girl's interest so easily, this is great.'

I expanded on the theme and told her that all I wanted to do was to make little children happy if I could, and fortunately I could grant her wish with my magic wand and I would do that if she told me what it was that she wanted. We looked into each other's eyes. I looked into her beautiful, large dark brown eyes and she looked back at me.

I said, 'Darling Jasmine, is there something you would like to ask me before I get that magic wand?'

She excitedly said 'Yes', and she was full of animation. I knew that here I had a child who realised what was happening, even though she was only four and a bit, that I had won her confidence and that I could feel secure in the knowledge that whatever she said to me I could rely upon and that she would tell me her true feelings.

I said, 'Darling, what is it you would like to ask me?'

She said, 'Where did you get those tracks on your face?'

And if you look at the front cover of this book, you'll see why this just made my day.

# CHAPTER 11

# BEYOND CARE

WE WERE at the Vietnamese soup restaurant in Beamish Street, Campsie, seven of us sitting around a formica table eating soup and talking. The place had become a bit of a haven for me and my closest colleagues at Campsie, and on particularly harrowing days I'd adjourn for lunch a few minutes early, and my court monitor and clerk would know to round up the regular duty solicitors and a few staff and we'd be off for an el cheapo lunch. By now I had been more than a year at Campsie and, while I was very happy about how the care court was doing, I was still frustrated that there was so much cruelty and violence occurring and that, no matter how hard we all tried, there appeared to be no way the system could cope with it. I didn't have a simple answer myself, but I knew that ill-treated kids and their parents were treated like second-class citizens, and I was getting pretty sick of just seeing them go in one door and out the other, often to return.

For example, on that day I had placed into temporary care twelve-year-old Nancy, whose mother had tied her hands and feet with rope and beaten her with a tree branch. Nancy had been left with welt marks across her shoulders, both cheeks, legs and arms and her mother had received a shock when she realised she could lose her daughter forever.

I lectured and cajoled her and ordered that she seek help, reminding her that she had narrowly escaped criminal assault charges. Then I'd dealt with little three-year-old Pat, who had been assaulted by his mother's de facto. He had been badly bruised, had a cut to his eye, bite marks to his back and shoulder and bruising to his penis which had been twisted. His mother had been before me teary and feeling sorry for herself. The de facto was off the scene now, but I'd ordered reports before I decided whether Pat could safely go home.

I had also listened to progress reports about Elsa, a fifteen-year-old girl whose suffering had emerged after she confided to her doctor that her father had hit her on her head and upper body many times because she arrived late for work in his shop, a small, mixed business. Elsa had been unable to say whether this was with his open hand or fist because she had been cowering on the floor at the time. She had further claimed that her father threatened to kill her. Since the Department of Community Services had been called in, it had been revealed that for Elsa, this type of abuse had been frequent and going on for some time. The father had all his children working in his shop, even though some were younger than twelve. Elsa was looking much more relaxed with temporary foster parents, but there was a lot of work to be done with her family before they could be helped to solve their problems.

So after a morning like that a lunch at the restaurant, which boasted over fifty different types of soup, was particularly welcome. There were a couple of duty solicitors, a barrister who'd come in to represent a young girl who had been abused, my court monitor and the court registrar. One of the solicitors was Jack, who was on duty that day and had been working in children's courts for as long as I had. He was telling us, again, his favourite tale about a policeman—a young ocker guy who was ambitious and took his job very seriously. He was working at Glebe Court of Petty Sessions in the days when Jack and I were young solicitors. Jack was telling everyone of the day when the next defendant to be called was Hugh Ryan. The practice in court is for the court constable to go to the waiting room and call the defendant's name three times, which, on this day, he did. This young policemen's strong Aussie accent and the defendant's name didn't really mix, however, and he started calling out what sounded like 'U-rine'. And when it appeared there was no 'U-rine' after his first three goes, he called it out again three times. Finally, Hugh Ryan stood up, but by then the constable's efforts had been overheard in the courtroom, so that when the constable arrived back to announce, 'U-rine before the court, Your Worship', we were all in stitches at the Bar Table. The magistrate was trying very hard not to join in. The court constable glared at us for our insensitivity.

When Ryan had been dealt with, the next defendant was James Neil. The constable ushered James Neil into the courtroom. After asking him if he had a solicitor and on receiving a negative answer, the constable turned to the magistrate and said, 'Neil before the court Your Worship.' We were all startled when suddenly the defendant got on to his knees. The constable was looking at the magistrate, but when he turned around he saw the kneeling Mr Neil. His eyes popped. 'Get up you bloody fool,' he screamed. Well, that had finished us at the Bar Table! The magistrate had to leave the Bench and adjourn for morning tea-break, even though we'd only been sitting for twenty-five minutes.

Jack's tales brought back all my memories of Glebe and I recalled that back in those days I had long hair. I had been sitting in the courtroom just in front of the dock when the defendant, who had been charged with escaping lawful custody, grabbed my hair and jerked my head back. I thought I was being kidnapped or going to be held as a hostage. It turned out the poor man was having a fit!

After Glebe, the talk moved on to football and the British royal family—anything but the law. A few sage hands had warned me that no-one could deal with a constant parade of care cases and I did feel it was getting to me. I relied on these lunches to temporarily take my mind off work. Four days a week in the court was pretty frustrating—but I only had one day away from care, and that was when I sat at Lidcombe Children's Court hearing criminal cases.

I left the lawyers to it at the restaurant and was back on the dot of 2 p.m. I knew that before the court could resume, I would have to go through the reports that were coming in over the lunch hour. It took me twenty minutes or so to read them, but by that time my fellow lunchers had also arrived back and it was time to get on with it.

As I walked onto the Bench, the laughter, jokes and light-heartedness of the lunch hour seemed like days ago, and once again it was down to business. My first case after lunch was of baby Peter, and I didn't like the sound of it at all. The Department of Community Services solicitor read the facts and handed me the medical report:

> *Peter was first notified as a child at risk when his mother took him to a local medical centre which immediately referred him to hospital. Hospital medical staff found Peter had multiple fractures to his arms and ribs of various ages, multiple bruises to his body, severe swelling of both eyes with conjunctivitis, gross nappy rash, what appeared to be human bite marks to various parts of his body and various other abrasions to his head and body. Peter was also dehydrated and medical staff believed he showed signs of recent weight loss.*

I thought I had seen the worst of human behaviour but my God, there was always more of it out there. I glanced up from reading the medical report and looked down from the Bench at the mother of this little nine-month-old baby who had been close to death and had had to be put on a morphine drip to help ease his pain. Nine months old! His mother sat there next to her solicitor with her hands, palms down, on the seat under her legs, staring at the floor. She looked half-starved herself, this undernourished, pale, poorly dressed twenty-four-year-old woman with long, lank hair and a long, lank face. She wore a pair of black leggings with a blue T-shirt over the top and a pair of thongs. It didn't help her appearance that she had been brought here to Campsie in a prison van from the women's detention centre at Mullawa where she had been remanded in custody. She had been charged with neglecting her baby, exposing and abandoning a child under two, and concealing a serious offence. She was due to face a magistrate's court on the criminal charges, but was here at Campsie so I could decide what to do with Peter in the immediate future. To be honest, when I read that report, I didn't care much about what happened to his pathetic mother. It was Peter I cared for. And there was another factor. This woman was already pregnant again. If she had allowed this to happen to Peter, what in heaven's name was going to happen to the unborn baby?

Peter's father was also behind bars. He was in Long Bay Gaol facing charges similar to those faced by his de facto wife. He didn't even want to be involved in these Children's Court proceedings and had officially withdrawn. He could, of course, have applied for custody of Peter when he got out of gaol but even he knew that the neglect and abuse was so severe that there was no chance. I strongly suspected that he probably didn't care.

Even the blue and pink of the decor and the Laura Ashley wall fabric failed to take the chill off the case I was hearing.

I shook my head and signalled to the department's solicitor with my right hand. I wanted to hear for myself what had happened and said it was time to hear from the district officer who had care of Peter's case. I did complain about some district officers, but the fact is that they had seen as much cruelty as I had and I don't know how many of them kept going. Some were angels. Hard-working angels.

This district officer was Alice, and she was sworn in and took a seat at the witness table.

She had been called by a doctor at a children's hospital the previous night, as soon as Peter had been presented. Everyone at the hospital involved in the case knew that this was a particularly horrid case of child abuse, but the mother was admitting nothing. In a corridor at the hospital, she told Alice that three days previously, Peter had fallen off a bed in the flat where the family lived.

'The mother told me,' said Alice, her voice quivering with emotion, 'that she had not taken him to a doctor because she felt he was all right and he hadn't appeared concussed.

'When asked about his eyes, the mother said she had only noticed they were infected two days previously and had treated them herself by bathing them in salt water.' Salt water! Every adult in the court flinched.

After years of bitter experience I knew that the excuse given by those who abused their children, and who caused broken ribs or arms or any other serious injury, was that the child had 'fallen off a bed'. It may only have been a mattress lying on the floor, but that was how it was alleged it had occurred.

Well, here it was being used again in Peter's case, and neither the doctors nor the district officer, Alice, had believed a word of the story.

As Alice didn't believe a word of it and, due to the unsatisfactory explanation, the extent of the serious injuries and the fact that his mother had not sought any help for him, care of Peter had been assumed under Section 62 of the *Children (Care and Protection) Act 1987*.

I never became hardened to the stories of these abused children, but I sometimes wondered if because I had heard so many of the tall tales their mothers and fathers told repeatedly, I had become unforgiving. It was like a broken record, time and again. They always said the injuries were accidental.

I was appalled by this miserable woman sitting before me. After more evidence from Alice it appeared she would leave Peter with the de facto husband while she went out and drank, or got drugs or other men. And she really couldn't care about the baby. She just sat there before me wanting this case over and done with as soon as possible. But she wasn't going to get her wish. Because of the extent of the injuries and the fact that no one could tell if his injuries would lead to permanent blindness or brain damage, a major investigation was started. In fact, she appeared before me another four times over the subsequent two months.

This is the picture that emerged from those four hearings: Peter had remained for three weeks before he had been allowed to go to a new home with foster parents. While in hospital, examinations on his eyes showed he would be permanently blind in his left eye due to severe, untreated conjunctivitis. He had only limited vision in his right eye due to a cataract and haemorrhaging likely to have been caused by a blow to the eye. His vision in that eye was being carefully monitored and was likely to improve with time.

Peter had even had a CAT scan in hospital because doctors feared at one time he might have had fluid on the brain, which would have required a shunt to be inserted. Fortunately, that was not the case.

Alice had spent quite a bit of time on the case and had also looked into the mother's background. She was one of the youngest in a family of fifteen children and had grown up in a country town. Before she was ten, her mother had left the family and the children had been raised by one another and by their father, an alcoholic. From the age of fifteen, she had been in a relationship for five years with a man who had been extremely violent towards her. Then she had met the man who was to be the father of her children, and he had helped her escape from the violent relationship. Tragically for her son, it was a case of out of the frying pan into the fire, I thought to myself.

In an attempt to find work, they had moved from the country town to Sydney just about six weeks before Peter was taken into hospital. They had been living in the small flat, but the father had been unable to get a job.

In formal interviews with Alice the mother told one story after another. She had also been interviewed by crisis care workers and the police. At first she had been adamant that her de facto would not have hurt Peter and told the story about the fall from the flat bed.

Then she claimed that the de facto had little by little stopped her seeing Peter over the four weeks they lived in the flat. She had been allowed to leave the flat only to buy groceries, she said, and when asked why she didn't get help for Peter while she was out, her answer was that her life had been threatened and she was scared.

She claimed not to have been able to see her son for the last week in the flat because her de facto husband had put up a 'screen', using a blanket hanging from the top bunk over the bottom bunk where Peter had been kept. According to the mother, the baby had not been moved off the bunk for that whole week. Her de facto had even slept with Peter every night.

In one interview, which was given to me by way of statement, Alice asked, 'Didn't you hear Peter screaming, crying?' which was something I wanted to know as well.

'Yeah, I'd hear him moaning and I said, "Is he okay, you're not hurting him, are you?" and he said, "No, he's just stirring",' the mother had replied.

She said her de facto had taken over the care of their son when they came to Sydney, telling her not to worry and to get some rest and look after the baby she was carrying. This couldn't possibly be the same caring, sharing man who had beaten his son to within an inch of his life, I thought!

The mother looked up just once or twice while I was hearing all this. She could spin a good tale, I thought, and I didn't believe it any more than the district officer obviously had. The truth was probably somewhere down the middle, a combination of the de facto dishing out the injuries, possibly with little thought as to the consequences, and the mother just abandoning her child.

The district officer had said to her, 'Peter was close to death. He had so many injuries that he must have been in great pain for at least the last four weeks before he got to hospital. It's hard to believe that when you were able to see him a week before he went to hospital, that you didn't notice any of his injuries.'

The mother's answer was that her de facto had taken control of everything. Once when she had pulled the screen up to see her son in the bunk, he had told her not to look because it was too upsetting, she said.

'It's just his eyes,' she claimed the de facto had said.

Despite her avowed concerns, her de facto had walked out in the morning after a row, but it was not until that evening, and then only on the prompting of friends, that she took Peter to the hospital.

'I didn't know where to go, I didn't know no-one. I was crook myself, spewing. Thank God my friends came. Eventually I would have done something. I knew one thing, I had to get help for Peter,' she had told the officer.

The district officer had said to her, 'Do you realise his injuries were life-threatening?'

'Yes, I do, that's fucking terrible, terrible that is. I'd better get him back, I'll fight for him. I wouldn't hurt my baby,' the mother had replied.

I looked at this young woman sitting before me and

thought again, that a lot of people have babies for all the wrong reasons. I don't believe it is true that young mothers necessarily make bad mothers. I do believe though that no matter what a mother's age, unless she is prepared to forego a lot of good times and self-indulgence for the next sixteen years, especially if she is on her own or with a temporary partner, then she should think very seriously before embarking on motherhood. If it's between 'the kid' and having a good time, then all too often the latter will win out. But the fact remains that most mothers would die rather than let anything happen to their babies. But occasionally, like the person who was before me, a mother does not bond with her child. Mothers who come from dysfunctional families with bad life experiences and who never bonded to their own mother, seem to find it harder to make the attachment to their own child. And it is quite stunning that people who know they can't look after babies properly often keep on having them. They also often find it difficult, as this woman had, to form long-term relationships with partners. But all of that is no excuse for cruelty like this.

Peter's mother stood little chance of getting him back at all, in my opinion, and certainly no chance while she was in Mullawa and had these criminal charges coming up. The problem for Peter was that he needed to be near a hospital because of his medical conditions. His prognosis was still unclear, as doctors had no idea what would be the long-term effects of his beatings and neglect. He had been with a foster family, but more long-term care was needed because at the least, the mother was going to be on remand for a while yet.

The district officer had found a family willing to take the baby on a long-term basis. They had three children, aged twelve, sixteen and eighteen years and lived near a hospital where he could get the care he so badly needed. He also needed a lot of love and affection, I thought. Hugs and cuddles had evidently been lacking in his short life. I hoped that the three children of the proposed foster parents were prepared for their mother and their father to be preoccupied with little Peter. They had a difficult road ahead of them.

It is harder to be a long-term foster parent than a parent, I believe, because of all the uncertainty it can bring. When I made a child a ward, it could be for a set time period, such as twelve months or two years, or until the child reached the age of sixteen. Even if the time period is fixed, however, it does not prevent the natural parents of the child making numerous applications to the court for the restoration of custody. Each time the foster parent, who has put in a lot of time, effort and love into caring for the child, let alone money, can very easily lose them. Unlike the parents, they don't always get the chance to appear in the witness box to put their side of things. They have to rely on what the district officer says about what improvement they have seen in the child. Yet at the same time, a district officer must tell the truth, and if they have seen an improvement in the behaviour of a ward's natural parents, it's up to them to tell the court. It is something foster parents have to accept when they take on the job of foster parenting. But it doesn't make handing over a child they love to parents who might again abuse them any easier.

Personally I wanted to see the end of wardship, and still do. I would prefer to see a form of 'guardianship' under which the child can go to foster parents for say, twelve months, with the involvement of the natural parents so the child remains in touch with them. At the same time the natural parents can learn from the foster parents and professional workers how to take care of their child. If the parents choose not to be involved, or show a lack of interest during the time they are supposed to be involved, then the child would be put into the care of those foster parents for a definite period of time. After two years, the foster parents should be able to adopt the child by way of 'open adoption'.

'Open adoption' means that the adoptive parents have the day-to-day care of the child, including schooling and medical welfare, but the natural parent is not denied agreed contact with the child. Too many children are damaged forever going from one short-term foster placement to another while mum or dad goes through drug rehabilitation or seeks proper medical care for a psychiatric condition. These children have the same rights as their parents and should be given a chance to get on with their lives. If you have people who are prepared to love and give these children not only a home but the benefit of a secure and stable life, then that's where the child should be. When the child is in its teens or old enough to make its own decision, then let them decide if they want to spend more time with their natural parents. So many times I have heard parents say, '*It's my kid.*' I do not believe that any of us own another human being. I can't subscribe to keeping a child on a shelf till Mum or Dad does or doesn't get their act together and properly provide for their children, not in a monetary sense, but with love and care and nourishment.

I could only make a wardship order if I was satisfied that by doing so, there would be a 'significant improvement' in the standard of care being given to the child. I felt I could not be satisfied of that unless I had a report on the foster parents, or unless I met them. I preferred to meet them wherever possible. I not only annoyed but angered some children's services by refusing to make a wardship order because I wasn't satisfied that there would be this 'significant improvement'. Sometimes I would be told that because of difficulties with a particular child, for behavioural, health, psychiatric, or psychological reasons, no foster parents had yet been found. But as soon as I made an order of wardship it would be easier to find foster parents. I never could see the logic in that and accordingly, I never made a child a ward unless I knew where the child was going.

Alice, Peter's district officer, knew my thoughts on this and knew I liked to see the foster parents sitting in court so I could see who I was sending the child to and could talk to them about it. She told me that the foster parents were prepared to come along to court on whatever day I required them. On the last day I dealt with Peter's case the foster parents came to court and brought their three children with them, and I was impressed. Peter was eventually to go and stay with them under a wardship order that he remain until the age of sixteen.

As Alice left the court, and my involvement with Peter ceased, I reflected that I wished there were foster parents for some of the adults I had to deal with. Adults like Annie and Bruce, who were two of my 'regulars' at Campsie.

I had been seeing this couple for several months and knew the family well. Annie and Bruce were both intellectually impaired and had three daughters, aged six, four and two years. The family had come before me because the district officers felt they had been helping them for as long as they could and now they needed some other assistance. Annie had become belligerent towards them and they felt that she had given up listening to them. It was not for Annie and Bruce that they were concerned, but for their daughters. It was not thought the children were intellectually disabled, but more that they lacked stimulation and were not developing as well as they should be.

Bruce was not as intellectually impaired as his wife, although he would never be able to get a driver's licence, and his working life was limited to menial tasks. Annie was unable to cope with money, she couldn't shop and she couldn't save. She would often forget to dress her children, or even to get out of bed.

They were, however, distraught to find themselves in court and when they had first come before me several months earlier, Annie had been sobbing and looking at every person around that courtroom for sympathy. She was only in her early thirties but looked as if she were in her late forties. She was unkempt and unwashed. Annie and Bruce were childish in the way they interacted with each other. Annie was totally unrestrained, arguing with Bruce one moment and kissing him the next as the emotion swept over her. The next minute, however, she could just as easily be hitting him.

I had immediately sent their three daughters out of the room with one of the court officers because I didn't want them to see their mother so distressed.

'Annie,' I said, 'my role is to do my utmost to keep your children with you. With your cooperation, I will do everything I can to that end. There is no evidence of abuse, either physical or sexual.

'You can take your children home with you but you will need to accept some help.' Help for Annie was not easy. She needed to learn to shop and to handle money. She needed help to get into a routine at home so she would learn to get out of bed, care for her children and run the house. The couple was paying an exorbitant rent for a two-bedroom unit, so I needed the cooperation of the Housing Commission to get them a cheaper place to live.

I wanted the two-year-old, Susie, to go to a local health nurse regularly, and I told Annie that she was going to have to take Susie to the area health clinic and then to preschool one day a week for stimulation. Laura, who was four, had to attend kindergarten at least three days a week and had to turn up properly dressed. Meanwhile Jane was to go to school every day with her packed lunch and be properly dressed, because some days she had been turning up at school wearing her pyjamas. Because Annie and Bruce were illiterate, Jane's school was to be advised that if there were any function or excursion on at the school, they either had to telephone or visit her parents, or arrange for a district officer to do so, to make sure that Jane did not miss out on anything.

That first time I adjourned the matter for four weeks, and Annie and Bruce went home with their three daughters while I attempted to plug in some assistance for them. As they left the court, Annie was thrilled. She laughed and spoke to everybody in court, telling them that it was a good day.

When they came back to court a month later, I was told that Bruce had taken Susie regularly to the area health clinic and had an attendance card to prove it. Three days a week he took Laura himself to make sure she went to kindergarten, often carrying her the two kilometres each way. Jane had been taken to school by Annie most mornings, but not all, and although she was not always clean, it was obvious that Annie was making an effort. I was so pleased that things appeared to be working out and praised them highly. They were both glowing.

Then the district officer reported that the Housing Commission said there was a two-year waiting list for accommodation and they couldn't jump the queue. I was told that home service could only last a few months, but that they would make every effort to have Annie organised by then. The Salvation Army was helping out with meals, but they could not give the court an undertaking that this could continue long term. The people from the St Vincent de Paul Society were able to draw up a financial plan and would do their best to supervise the couple but again, they could not, through any fault of their own, put in the intensive hours that Annie and Bruce needed.

I had adjourned the matter for another four weeks, hoping that a personal plea from me could do some good with the Housing Commission, Homecare, the Salvation Army and St Vincent de Paul.

But just two weeks later Annie and Bruce were back before me. Jane had not been to school, Laura had been to kindergarten only once and only little Susie was having the attention I thought she required. The fridge in their home was empty of everything but twelve bottles of tomato sauce, and Annie had refused to let anyone either into the house or to help in any way. She and Bruce had been fighting in front of their children. It was obvious that this was having a detrimental effect on the three girls and could not go on. I thought I would try a different tack.

I called Annie over to the Bench and lent across to her.

'I want you to believe me when I say to you that I do not intend to deprive you of your children permanently. Annie, do you know what that means?' I asked.

Annie said she thought she understood.

I told her that the children would not be going home with them that day. 'But I am saying that in a few weeks, I am hoping that they will be back with you,' I said.

Annie sobbed and Bruce put his arm around her, but they said they understood and left the court quietly.

The girls went to a foster home and I ordered psychological assessments on each of them. I asked the district officers to prepare a detailed report for me as to what they felt the department could offer this family in an effort to keep them together.

Just over a week later, however, the matter was back before me. Annie had refused to work with any of the district officers, even those she had known for a long time. Other officers had tried in case there was a personality problem, but she would not talk to any of them. She had even decided to lock out the Salvation Army. Annie had become obstinate and threatening. While we were all turning cartwheels to help her, she felt threatened. She feared she was once again losing control of her life and of her children. Annie had also become angry with me and called me a few choice names which questioned my morals and my parentage. I told her I would give her a fortnight to change her attitude and that I didn't care if she didn't like me, but she had to cooperate with the people who were trying desperately to help her.

Although it had taken months to get to this stage, as Annie and Bruce walked into court that afternoon, I think they knew as well as I did that this final hearing was not going to take long. When it got to this point, I had to concentrate on the children and what was in their best interests. Was it in their best interests to stay with a mother and father who, even if they did try their utmost, would never be able to bring their children to their full potential? Parents who would probably make their children the butt of every cruel joke at school and the subject of pity because they would turn up not dressed properly and dirty.

I had read the reports over the past fortnight; nothing had changed. Annie was still not cooperating and had become even more unkempt and disorganised, yet my heart went out to her. What she needed was help. This was going to be one of the hardest decisions I had ever made and I felt very sad; sad and helpless. I had no alternative but to commit the three girls to wardship for their own welfare. When I told Annie this, she began to sob and scream. Bruce cried a little, but he was quiet and shook his head. He told Annie to shut up and turned to her.

'I told you this would happen. It's all your fault,' he said to her.

I sat there and watched as they left the court with their solicitors. Annie was inconsolable. When she got to the door of the court she turned around, pointed at me and her voice was shaking as she said, 'You promised. You promised me I would keep my babies.'

And of course she was right. I had made that promise and I had broken it. In the end I had no choice.

For me, that was the beginning of the end of my days as a

magistrate, because no matter how hard we tried, not the federal Government, the state Government nor any of the local governments were doing enough to keep families together. People like Bruce and Annie had to rely on charity as the system couldn't help them.

After Annie shouted at me through her tears, she slammed the door of the court and left my life. But she didn't really. She remained firmly in my thoughts, and I hated the fact that wardship was the only alternative for her problems. I sat in my chambers that night and contemplated my life. I was sixty-three, and although I'd seen and been through a lot, I felt I had not achieved enough to help children and families, and as long as I sat on the Bench that state of affairs would continue. It was on that day I decided to quit.

CHAPTER 12

# THE FINAL CHAPTER (FOR NOW, ANYWAY…)

MY DECISION to step down from the Bench was not easy. I could still feel the thrill and the pride of the day when I was appointed to the Bench, and it really seemed like yesterday, and it still does. But of course it wasn't yesterday and a lot of time has passed since then and now. Fourteen years, to be exact. There comes a time, however, when you know you have had enough; when you have to write the last chapter and close the book, and that day for me as a magistrate came one day early in May 1994. On the morning of that day, my hand was shaking when I picked up the phone and dialled Rod Blackmore, the Chief Magistrate of the Children's Court. I had always liked Rod. He was a friend as well as a boss and was a sort of judicial soul mate when it came to the welfare of kids. He was, I knew, as frustrated as I was with the lack of funding and support for troubled kids. But he was far more resilient and able to take it and, in my mind, was the most outstanding senior magistrate the court had known. Rod was exceptionally dedicated and worked extraordinary hours, and if he had chosen to be an independent solicitor, could easily have earned a multiple of his comparatively small salary as Chief Children's Magistrate. As for me, I had never aspired to become Chief Magistrate. With that job goes the essential, but extremely boring meetings with government agencies and the hours of administration—as well as sitting as a children's magistrate. I just didn't have the patience that Rod obviously had before his retirement in 1995.

I had confided in a few of my close friends and told them I was going to resign. Invariably the response was, 'Sure Barb,' and I guess I really didn't believe it myself until the time came to put it firmly on the record.

I took a deep breath. 'G'day Rod, it's Barb. Rod, I'm going to resign.'

There was a pause, and then the sound of Rod's friendly voice, 'Barb, why would you want to do that?' God, I almost wavered.

But there was no point in beating around the bush. 'I've got to tell you that I think I've become some form of human rubber stamp.

'I've just really had it and I feel I'm getting nowhere. I'd really hoped Campsie Care Court could bring about change, but really nothing has changed. Christ, Campsie is the only court of its kind and they still can't see what it's all about. You'd think they'd make some political mileage out of it.

'In crime, we have next to no alternatives. In care, the support is getting less and less, rather than more and more.

'I really want to do something about it, and the only way is to talk. But I feel I'm embarrassing everyone with all the media coverage.'

'You've never embarrassed me, Barb,' he said. Another pause, then he went on.

'There's a lot of talk from the usual quarters about new plans and schemes and things, but, yep, you're right. I can see why you're going.'

Rod didn't know how close I came to withdrawing my resignation, and if I had I guess I'd still be on the Bench, still sending kids to institutions, still weeping at the suffering of babies at the hands of pathetic parents, knowing that there was no effective system to help them. But I felt I had a job to do, and I could do it better by not being publicly fettered by the constraints of being a magistrate.

My last day on the Bench was 29 June, my birthday, and lots of my colleagues turned up to watch my final cases. There were only three or four cases listed for that last morning, but two of them turned out to be extraordinarily indicative of what I'd seen over the years. First, a little Muslim girl came in to court with her district officer. She was nine years old, and had been in foster care for a month. I had placed her there as soon as her case had come before me, as her mother had refused to give me a guarantee that she would protect her daughter from her brute of a husband and the girl's father. The little girl had come home from school one day without her cardigan, having left it in the library. The father's response was to beat her with a belt, until her back bled. The next day, a teacher noticed the injuries and reported it to the department. Once again, the kind of difficult decision I had been constantly faced with. Should I send the girl home to the possibility of further violence, or make her a ward, which would deprive her of every child's right to live with its natural parents?

The girl's solicitor said the child wanted to say something to me. The girl, her dark hair and eyes without the glow of natural health for a child that age, walked up to the Bench, and I leant down to listen. I knew that the family who had been looking after her in foster care were not Muslim, and so she had probably been subjected to a major change in culture and diet. She whispered, ever so softly, 'Please can I go home today?'

I didn't really know if the girl had been coached to ask this—she certainly would have seen her natural parents during her time in care, and perhaps there might have been some sort of coaching for the occasion.

'Are you sure that's what you want, darling?' I asked her.

'Yes,' was the reply, and she walked back to her seat. The father was sitting behind his solicitor, with a stony face and nothing to indicate any remorse. The mother, dressed in her grey traditional garb, just glared at me.

I was angry, and so was she, but at least it was my courtroom and I had the upper hand. I felt I had no choice but to send the girl home, but not without letting the family know their behaviour would not be accepted.

I yelled, and I make no apology for it, 'This country will accept your religion, the way you dress, your music, your food, but it will not accept cruelty to children.

'There is no place for it in Australia. And if it comes to my attention that you have laid a finger on this little girl again, you will have to answer to an assault charge in another court.

'But your daughter, through all of this, still loves you both and she wants to go home with you and I'll let her go home under strict conditions. One of them is that you will attend the Arabic Welfare Association and have counselling in relation to the punishment you dish out to your daughters.'

The mother started screaming in a high-pitched whine, 'You don't understand. I would have received this treatment. My mother would have received this treatment.'

I interrupted and said, 'Exactly, and that's why it's stopping today.'

I really felt like saying, 'You can walk at three paces behind him if you like, but this girl is going to walk with her head held high', but I left it there.

What a finish to my career! My last major decision was about a little fellow who had been taken away from his mother, with her consent, because she was schizophrenic and he was hyperactive. But at that time she never dreamt that the separation would be for ten months and there would be any obstacles to him being returned to her. Once again the only mistake the mother had made was to cry for help. The child was keen to go home and the mother was even keener to have him. The department, however, wanted him to stay in Minali, an institutional home where wards remain until suitable accommodation is found for them—if, indeed, it ever is.

'Why?' I asked the department's solicitor.

'Because we want to conduct further investigations,' she said.

I glanced down at the little boy's file. It was almost twelve centimetres thick! All those reports and not one line of a decision.

'More investigation? You're joking,' I said, and with the stroke of a pen I returned the boy to his mother.

Yep, I thought to myself, maybe my life on the Bench hasn't been entirely unproductive when there are moments like this.

And really, it hadn't been unproductive at all. That morning's proceedings, and my life as a magistrate, finished before lunch. Just before I stepped from the Bench for the last time, one of the solicitors asked for permission to approach the Bench.

'Granted,' I said, and Ted Bramble, one of the most experienced juvenile lawyers around, brought to the Bench one of the biggest bunches of flowers I had seen. As the tears clouded my appreciation of their bright colours, the court officer called out, in a break of format, 'All rise. The court of Barbara Holborow, Juvenile Magistrate, is closed.' That night, after the first of quite a few farewell parties, I thought of what I had experienced, what I had achieved, and what I had failed at. And I thought as well of the many characters who had come in and out of my life and would become part of my book. Characters you have now shared with me.

I suppose one of my biggest successes came, indirectly, through Mike, the eighteen-year-old boy I talked about in the first chapter, and whom I had to send to an adult gaol despite the fact that he was almost certain to be sexually and emotionally brutalised there. I have never been able to bring myself to find out what happened to him—I guess I really don't want to know. I do know that in the prison van taking him to Long Bay Gaol, he did threaten to commit suicide. I have heard he's now in a psychiatric institution. That case really galvanised me to do something publicly to help get a gaol, or a section of a gaol, where kids like Mike, who are in the netherworld between boyhood and manhood, could be housed with one another, rather than letting the old lags get their hands on them and without them being able to influence younger children. I had been pushing for years both publicly and privately for a place like this. Parklea Gaol, in Sydney's outer west, had opened in November 1983 as a prison for some of the state's most hardened offenders. In the early 1990s, with no fanfare, the prison quietly changed its policy to provide a place for young offenders such as Mike. They are now admitted into Parklea where they are able to spend their time with no other prisoners except 18- to 25-year-olds and first offenders. This was what I had been hoping for.

And this is what I know about some of the other kids from previous chapters. Four months after I resigned, I read in the paper that Pete, the boy who said he had stolen his last car after appearing before me in Minda with virtually his whole body in plaster, had been killed, not in a police chase but in a stolen vehicle all the same. It was on an unfamiliar dirt road in the country. Not only did he kill himself but he also killed a female passenger in the back seat. Both the others riding in the car with him were critically ill and if they survived, they would be disabled forever due to their head injuries. It is almost impossible to convince young people like him that they are not invincible, not immortal and that they can die and that, although they have wonderful reflexes, they do not have the experience necessary to deal with every eventuality. And, more often than not, they're not in a safe car. It almost seems as if they have a death wish.

There was Dimitri, the young Greek boy with the loving parents, who had bashed a man because he was gay. I had to commit him to a higher court, and I read subsequently that he had been given a heavy sentence and may even now still be in jail.

Bill, the boy racer who gave me that 'hot' snack food when I was feeling sorry for myself—who still touches me to this day because of his statement that I was 'his family'—must be twenty-six now. When *Sixty Minutes* did a follow-up program on me, which included filming on my final day, the producer tracked down Bill in gaol and asked if he would participate in the story. Bill told him he was worried that, if it were known that he had a friend who was a magistrate, he'd be in for a bashing or two. I told the producer, 'Please just forget about Bill. His life has been hard enough without me adding to the problems.'

Poor old Jocelyn, the frumpish young thing who gave everyone a hard time, ended up at the Pink Pussycat, a nightclub in Sydney's Kings Cross, working as a stripper. I know little more than that. I wonder if she ever went home. There were a lot like Jocelyn, unfortunately.

And I suppose Issie's mother got someone to clean the swimming pool. I do know that she and her husband ultimately divorced and remarried. Issie went to live with her mother's sister, and as far as I know she was very happy there.

Remember those Vietnamese kids who would appear before me with the five tattoos on their hands? One of them, Tri Minh Tran, rose through the ranks of his fellow gang members to become the leader of the 5T gang. He died the way he lived—he was murdered on 7 August 1995 in an apparent leadership fight. When he died in a hail of bullets in his Cabramatta unit, Tran was just twenty years old but had two children—and had beaten two murder charges which had been laid against him by the age of seventeen.

I seem to know more about the bad news stories than the good news ones because, paradoxically, a measure of my success was that a child would never come before me again. Snowy, the little runaway who slept with his dog Bruce Lee in a clothes bin is a good example. I never saw him again and that's wonderful. I hope Snowy and Bruce are still good mates.

I have over the years, however, received letters and photographs from other children. One Vietnamese boy, who came before me for just about every petty crime imaginable, later wrote that he himself wanted to write a book. He wanted to call it *Life's Hard—Why Make It Harder*? He wrote to me with some passion about his time in the Yasmar Detention Centre:

> *I was put into isolation for eight hours, and while I was in there they gave me a letter from my parents which I read and some things striked [sic] my mind.*
>
> *It was like being woken up from a bad dream. My parents told me they have never given up hope on me and they always loved me, no matter what I did in the past.*
>
> *I had plenty of time to think about what I had been doing and how much I had hurt my family and loved ones ... I am turning eighteen soon and I do not want to get into any more trouble.*

And there were other times that made it all worthwhile. As I write this, I'm looking at the latest photographs of three sisters. When I first met them in 1988, one was two, one was six and one was nine. Their mother had gone overseas and when she returned she made no provision for her children. Her whereabouts were unknown, and so the children came before me and the grandmother asked if she could take care of them. The kids were understandably puzzled and miserable and the grandmother apprehensive, but over the years she wrote to me regularly and included photos of the girls. This latest photograph is one of a happy, thriving, vibrant trio of young girls standing in front of a big, bright Christmas tree. Their granny wrote:

> *(It) was taken before the school presentation night at which (the eldest) received five awards.*
>
> *Your decision made four people very happy. I would like to take this opportunity to thank you for making that happiness possible.*

And now that we're getting to the end of this book, a couple of issues addressing other relevant factors.

There has been much publicity about the Wood Royal Commission and paedophilia, but I really didn't see much of the problem of paedophilia in my court. As early as 1983, I became aware of young boys working as male prostitutes in the area called The Wall, opposite St Vincents Hospital at Darlinghurst. I rarely saw any of these kids because of my catchment area—they were in the eastern suburbs and so would appear in another Children's Court, Bidura. I would have, however, seen half a dozen, maybe ten, of these young boys and I can honestly say that they weren't asking for help. They weren't asking for a change of lifestyle and if I tried to draw them out by getting them to talk about what I thought was their predicament, they shrugged their shoulders. If they were before me on a criminal matter and I made it a condition of their release that they weren't to return to that area, that condition was broken as early as that night. Some protested, when I said, 'Don't you realise how you're being used?' They protested that they were wearing clothes, good clothes, that they were being given money. I have to say that I didn't have any young boy come before me who was pleading for help to get out of the situation he was in. I joined with a very caring youth worker called Annie, who did her best to bring to the notice of the authorities, including the police, the plight of these boys at The Wall, but nobody listened to her at the time. Years later, of course, it has come to light that what she was saying then should have been investigated and action taken. She was fearless in her approach to paedophilia in that she wanted the paedophiles arrested and dealt with and the young people to receive counselling and support. I agreed that The Wall should not be permitted to continue in its operations—but it did.

I believe that there is room for a lot of improvement in the juvenile court system as it is today. One way would be to have juvenile magistrates travelling to country towns on circuit to relieve local magistrates from the formidable task of having to hear adults' and children's matters on the same day. This is especially so in care matters, which should be heard and dealt with as expeditiously as possible, and which require the expertise of an experienced Children's Court magistrate. But I am told that there has never been sufficient funding for this 'revolutionary' idea.

I believe there should be mediation sessions between parents and children when there is an alleged 'irretrievable breakdown'. These sessions should occur prior to the matter coming before the magistrate. Quite often in the Care Court there was the teenager (angry) and parents (angry and bewildered), and it really didn't need to get to that stage. I think there should be mediation, perhaps before a retired judge, magistrate, lawyer or other professional used to dealing with Children's Court matters.

And I also believe in the extensive use of sessions whereby the perpetrator of a crime should be forced to meet the victim of it. I know there have been trials of such schemes, and everything I hear about them is good. If a young person has stolen a handbag from an old lady, what do you think will really drive home the gravity of the offence? A day in court and a ticking off? Not at all.

If, however, the juveniles are forced to meet their victims, hear of their trauma, learn of their injuries, then I'm sure that in many cases it would have a huge impact. Perhaps, again, these sessions should be conducted in a semi-formal atmosphere before there is any court hearing. And I believe the victim should choose the punishment and, if the arbitrator thinks it reasonable, the proposal should be put before the magistrate for endorsement. If the perpetrator decides not to accept the punishment, or doesn't carry it out, then it would be time for a formal hearing.

Overall, what I am saying is that there has to be a stage between the police and the juvenile court system. A stage where attempts could be made to analyse and sort out what has gone wrong with a young person's life and how it could be fixed. There should be an intermediate step in our juvenile justice system between crime and punishment because with delinquent kids, we might just be able to rescue them before they become delinquent adults. It would, of course, cost money, but wouldn't it be worth it?

All in all, my life on the Bench has been one of bewilderment and frustration, happiness, bemusement and amusement, and one which I remain passionate about. But I can only see things getting worse for troubled kids. At the tip of the glacially proportioned iceberg of my concern about our juvenile justice system is, of course, money. I believe that those government departments with responsibility for children's welfare will never receive the resources they need. Juvenile justice has always been heard, and rarely seen.

But every day, out there, there is a cornucopia of disparate and desperate kids coming before the children's courts of this land, in heaps of trouble. And, if the public isn't interested, then the politicians certainly aren't. But I'll continue to make a noise, and I'll continue to fight until one day there are major changes. I promise you.